Obama's Great Education Lie

D1714363

by
John Loase

Obama's Great Education Lie

Copyright © 2012, by John Loase.

FIRST SUNBURY PRESS EDITION
Printed in the United States of America
April 2012

Trade paperback ISBN: 978-1-620060-39-1

Published by:
Sunbury Press
Camp Hill, PA
www.sunburypress.com

Camp Hill, Pennsylvania   USA

ACKNOWLEDGMENTS

Sigfluence is a word invented by me in 1984 and means significant, long-term positive influence. It is impossible to thank all my sigfluencers, but let me begin.

The late Burdette Graham, who tragically lost his life in an unjust war, was a key influence in all my ten books. Somehow we humans can turn great pain into creative endeavors.

My wonderful ninth grade teachers, Mary O'Connor Reynolds and Louis Rotando, were instrumental in my earning the first and last doctorate in Mathematics (emphasis Statistics) and Psychology (emphasis Measurement, Research and Evaluation) awarded by Columbia University Teachers College under the inspiring mentorship of the late Dr. Rchard Wolf and Dr. Bruce Vogeli.

This book is based on my experience of forty-two years of teaching. I have taught in Savage Inequality secondary schools (read Jonathan Kozol's book *Savage Inequality*), Horace Mann (an elite private high school), and college -remedial level through and including masters and Ph. D. I decided to write this work last spring, when I read about President Obama's speech at the University of Texas-Austin. He led the audience to believe that America could improve to #1 ranking in college graduation rates by 2020. I was very disappointed by this bald faced lie. However, the lie inspired this book. It is time to transform American education. But first, we have to face our collective national denial, neglect, and lies that have landed us closer to the bottom than the top in international educational rankings.

It is timely to transform education in America. My latest book, The Sigfluence Generation, revealed the huge Potential and Need for our Millennials to affect sigfluence. If young people can change the government in Egypt, our 18-25 year olds can positively transform American education. However, they need partnership and guidance from Baby

Boomers in order to avoid our mistakes and employ wisdom in an educational revolution.

I would like to express my deep gratitude to Mrs.Barbara Boyce for her extraordinary skill and patience in the typing and revising of ten books over the past three decades.

For Burdette

"My friend, I've been lying all my life. The most difficult thing in life is to live and not lie and not believe one's own lie."[1]

Fyoder Dostoevsky, *Demons*

INTRODUCTION

President Obama inspired this book. Sadly, his speech at the University of Texas at Austin, in which he urged the United States to retake the #1 position in college graduation rates by 2020, was a great lie. Given the fact that he is a brilliant man, he must be acutely aware that our current economic and job crisis will likely plunge us even deeper into an educational quagmire by the year 2020. I am a supporter of President Obama, but as a scholarly person I detest bald faced lies. Unless we alter course, we are likely to be closer to the bottom, #36, than the top #1.

One of my colleague's believes that President Obama's statement about rising to the top of the world in college graduation rates by 2020 was a goal, not a lie, but I disagree. The second definition of lie in The Unabridged Random House Dictionary (Second Edition) is:

"something intended or serving to convey a false impression."

President Obama tried to convey the impression that a goal, which is impossible given the current political, economic, and social climate, can truly be achieved. He purposely conveyed a false impression. He knew that the money, political will, and public support for a transformation of American education was not there. Therefore, he lied, and I became angry the moment I heard his lie. However, the outrage fueled this book.

President Obama has 300 million accomplices in his great lie. Americans talk a good game about education, but actions speak much louder than words. Education is grossly underfunded by our national, state and local government. Exemplary early childhood intervention programs, like Head Start and Pre-K, are constantly being

1

targeted for budget cuts. At the collegiate level, our gifted, but economically disadvantaged students have increasingly higher hurdles to overcome. It seems that we have abandoned the American dream for so many.

The deterioration of our educational infrastructure is largely invisible; however our slide from the best in the world in college completion rates to our present level of mediocrity requires each of us to face our own individual lies, which perpetuate the tragic educational plight. We are all accomplices to the politicians who insist that all is right in education, schools can do more with less, and lower taxes are a virtue. It is time for us to face these lies and reverse course.

When I started teaching in Yonkers forty-two years ago, I was expected to teach the New Math, a beautiful, highly rigorous creation by mathematicians. Due to the fact that I was well trained in math, I liked it. Unfortunately, the vast majority of my 180 students did not know the times table. To make matters worse, I only had twenty books, which I had to carry from room to room, having no room as a home base. I ended my first year of teaching wondering whether the goal of American education was really to educate, or to simply certify that the poor were failures, incapable of satisfactory work in college or the professions. Neither President Obama nor the American public really understands the obstacles confronting inner city education.

One needs only to read Jonathan Kozol's *Savage Inequality*, to understand the turmoil of day- to -day teaching in an economically disadvantaged school. After teaching in a Savage Inequality school for five years, I taught math at Horace Mann (an elite private school) and high school math at the middle class Saunders High School (Yonkers). Then I worked as a guidance counselor at the Savage Inequality Yonkers High School for seven years.

When Yonkers High School lost the charismatic and effective leadership of Principal Joe Farmer, chaos ensued and Yonkers High, an architectural wonder, was forced to close its doors. Students were assigned to new high schools, and I went on to teach college math for 28 years, chiefly at Westchester Community College (18 years) and presently as Chair of Math (10 years) at Concordia College, NY.

Throughout the course of my career, I have won a number of state and national awards for excellence in teaching. I was honored, but to be fair, no one can evaluate the effectiveness of one's teaching. The existence of an omniscient supervisor is another lie. We can safely screen out the 5 or 10% who have no place in the teaching profession, but that is all.

As a professor, I have nine published books. You can go to my website sigfluence.com and download my 8th book, *The Sigfluence Generation: Our Young People's Potential to Transform America*, for free. I invented the word sigfluence at the Harvard International Conference on Thinking 1984 in order to define significant, long-term, positive influence.

We deny sigfluence in our language, workplace, politics, and personal lives. My eight books on sigfluence are an attempt to reverse the neglect of our potential to affect lasting positive influence. In addition, this book calls on every individual to face their ever present lies and denial about the American educational system. We are all a part of the self-serving lie that we deeply support education. The truth is that we support what perpetuates our own family's privilege – little more.

In order to achieve balance, I interviewed the following key leaders and practitioners in education for this book:

1. President of SUNY Westchester Community College Dr. Joseph Hankin
2. New York State Superintendent of Yonkers-NY Bernard Pierorazio
3. Retired Army Officer, West Point Professor, and Dean Melvin Butts.
4. Principal Riverside High School Yonkers Steven Murphy
5. Assistant Principal of Riverside High School Yonkers Carol Baiocco
6. Master Teacher Riverside High School Maria Rodriguez
7. Tutor of TRIO Westchester Community College Gretchen Aufiero Loase

A detailed bio and rationale for each of these leaders can be found in Appendix A of this book. Every one of these individuals has been extremely generous with their time and counsel in granting interviews for this book. Our goal is to confront American denial with respect to the American educational system and contribute to a new era of educational excellence.

This brief introduction is intended to prepare you for an analysis of the great lies of American education. For Lie #7 (Education and Values and Religion Do Not Mix), I have interviewed several religious leaders and perused the written work of religious pioneers. The time has come to uncover the great American education lies and figure out some ways of fixing our broken system.

LIE #1 - America can become the world leader in college graduation rates by 2020.

There are lies, damned lies, and Statistics. Mark Twain popularized this phrase, attributing it to the 19th century British Prime Minister Benjamin Disraeli. We need Mark Twain to do justice to categorizing President Obama's grand lie that took place in August 2010, when he spoke at the University of Texas, Austin. University of Texas, Austin is a special place for me. They honored me with a national award for excellence in teaching several years ago. Sadly, no one from the University of Texas challenged President Obama's outrageous lie.

Superintendent Bernard P. Pierorazio

We live in denial and ignorance when we accept without question such a preposterous claim. Superintendent Bernard Pierorazio was recently named New York State Superintendent of the Year. During his tenure, he demonstrated great vision and zeal in turning education around in Yonkers. He introduced a pre-kindergarten through eighth grade model that has led to a dramatic increase in the high school graduation rate. He did away with middle schools (grades 6-8), which he found to be ineffective in urban centers. He also created smaller learning communities by consolidating the high schools. I taught with Bernard years ago, when I served as the guidance counselor at Yonkers High School. He was one of the finest teachers I have ever taught with. Yonkers was very wise in installing him as the Superintendent of Schools.

On May 13, 2011, Bernard announced the termination of over 700 employees and the elimination of the pre-kindergarten program. In Bernard's words:

"I liken it (the budget cuts) to Lego. You build an intricate Lego building and marvel, what a success.

5

That is what we built here (in Yonkers). A beautiful model. And a bully comes by and steps on it. Education is not valued in large urban centers."

If you do not feel like weeping when you read Superintendent Pierorazio's words, there is little reason for you to continue reading this book. I invented the word sigfluence twenty-eight years ago to define significant, long-term, positive influence. Visit my website - sigfluence.com and download my recent book, *The Sigfluence Generation: Our Young People's Potential to Transform America*. Our nation's youth want to transform the United States into a more caring and connected nation. We have to support leaders, like Superintendent Pierorazio, whose innovations and vision positively transform lives. Our nation presently has to be bludgeoned into a heightened sigfluence consciousness. Hundreds, perhaps thousands, of students' lives will be adversely affected by these tragic budget cuts. Education is the key to societal transformation, but it is currently crumbling, especially in economically disadvantaged areas.

Dr. Alan Greenspan

Over the past three decades, Federal Reserve Chair Dr. Alan Greenspan was one of the most powerful people in Washington. Let us forgive his neglect of regulation that led to the great financial crisis of 2008. Dr. Greenspan, along with countless others, failed to see the flimsiness of a financial system featuring derivatives that few, if any, understood.

On June 3, 2011, Dr. Greenspan was interviewed on Squawk Box. During this interview, he noted that in education, something bizarre is occurring between 4th grade, where our students excel, and 12th grade, where we are near the bottom in educational achievement. According to Dr. Greenspan money is not the issue, since we pay more per capita than other nations. He also wisely noted that poor education will cost the United States economy in the long-term. In his autobiography, Dr. Greenspan went on to say that our #1 national problem is poor achievement in Science and Mathematics. Not just a problem, but the #1 problem.

As this book develops, I will share several promising innovations in mathematics which could make substantial progress in healing the educational system, currently in need of intensive care.

Our educational problems are analogous to cancer. Cancer is treated in ways very specific to an individual's diagnosis. Similarly, education needs different interventions to cure the different cancers. We need an infusion of money to cure the cancer of current cuts to education. To remedy our pitiful national student participation in advanced mathematics, we need a separate strategy. President Obama cannot cure education by himself. We all need to be a part of a societal transformation. Americans must recognize that education is a long-term investment, the fruits of which may take decades to realize. We are not a long-term, reflective nation, but our 18-25 year olds have a dramatically high need and potential to affect sigfluence. There is hope.

Produce Eight Million Extra U.S. Graduates By 2020

Sarah Cunnane wrote a piece highlighting the reaction of educational experts to President Obama's rhetoric. No one believes that the United States can "retake the world lead" in global graduation rates. Phillip Altback, Director of the Center for International Higher Education at Boston College, was gentle in his assessment stating that "President Obama's target was 'not achievable' in the current economic conditions." The drive for increased graduation rates is contradicted by reality. California colleges and universities expect to turn away more than 100,000 students seeking college degrees as a result of their budget crises. Yonkers is not alone. Dr. Michael Kirst, emeritus Professor of Education at Stanford, said that eight million additional college graduates "would be tough even if everything were to remain the same," which it is not. According to Dr. Kirst, graduation rates are currently falling.[2]

President Obama's Tools Are Few

President Obama correctly identified the reasons for stagnation of the American rate of college graduation, including:

1. Rising costs.
Tuition and housing costs rose 439% from 1982 to 2008 compared with a 147% increase in median family income.

2. A disconnect between skills learned and skills needed.
In my eight books, I introduce covert bias as a fundamental concept underlying the gap between what professionals need and what colleges provide. Stay tuned. An entire Lie is devoted to this idea.

3. Dropout rates.
Superintendent Pierorazio was extremely proud of his 90% graduation rate for students benefitting from his pre-kindergarten - 8th grade initiative, and justifiably so. The Yonkers budget cuts may cut this exemplary success rate in half. Do we want the prison industry to be one of the growth industries in America? Crime is linked to the educational hopelessness of the underclass. "Gerald Lynch, President of John Jay College of Criminal Justice, advises America that the answers to our social problems are not just changes in the laws or courts or jails. In President Lynch's words:

"We must send signals on public policy. What makes the difference is changes in the social fabric of our society".

The Open Society Institute, created by George Soros, found that the majority of incarcerated prisoners came from low income, urban communities with underserved educational support. We pay for systemic inequality.

President of the National Center for Public Policy and Higher Education, Patrick Callan, believes that the money is just not there for President Obama's higher education plans. In Mr. Callan's words:

> "Obama had planned a fairly well-funded initiative incentivizing college completion rates, but he lost that money during the legislative process of health care reform."[3]

We need health care reform as well as incentives to increase college completion rates, not one or the other. We need a drastic societal transformation.

Aftershock

Greed and denial stand in the way of achieving President Obama's goal of the U.S. becoming #1 in the world in college graduation rates. In his recent book, *After-Shock*, Robert Reich reveals that in 2007 the richest 1% of Americans took in 24% of U.S. income. The last time this happened was in 1928, before the Great Depression.[4]

Some might object to Reich's analysis since he served in the perceived liberal Clinton administration as Secretary of Labor. However, Dr. Reich also served in the Ford and Carter administrations and President Clinton's economic tenure became the envy of conservative Republicans. Whether liberal or conservative, Dr. Reich has simply observed that we are reaching a level of unsustainable greed, refusing hope to an increasingly large set of fellow Americans.

Dr. Reich is not alone in this observation. Conservative New York Times columnist David Brooks instructs us that our structural problems are going unaddressed. He observes that "semi-crackpot, Donald Trump, was able to garner astonishing political stature" before his effort to be taken seriously as a presidential candidate imploded. Mr. Brooks predicts that new political forces will emerge from the brewing crisis that our structural problems will create.[5] Our young people have the potential and the need to affect sigfluence and usher in an era of caring and connection. However, they need partnership and mentorship from the baby boomers.

President of Westchester Community College Dr. Joseph Hankin

Twenty-eight years ago I was interviewed by Dr. Hankin for a position as Assistant Professor of Mathematics. I was offered the position, and accepted it with the intention of staying a few years and then moving on to a university doctoral position in Statistics and Educational/Psychological Measurement. Dr. Hankin and my mentor Professor Louis Rotando (math chair) provided me with opportunities for professional growth that I never could have imagined. I stayed at Westchester for nearly two decades. President Hankin was named one of the Best College Presidents by his peers. This is my tenth book, an outgrowth of Dr. Hankin's positive leadership.

Dr. Hankin cited enhanced access, which Westchester Community College has provided to people who otherwise may not have been able to go on to higher education, as his greatest career success. Year after year, his greatest challenge has been reaching groups like the economically disadvantaged, the underprivileged and the learning disabled.

Dr. Hankin has marshaled enormous resources, including 100 professors and staff into the Freshman Experience, which focuses on improving college rates of retention and graduation. The key to college success is fostering connections. Dr. Hankin cited TRIO as an extraordinary program. Students in TRIO are identified by 1) economic need; 2) remedial level; and 3) 1st generation college students. Three strikes and you are in, and, unlike baseball, TRIO hits a grand slam. Eighty-nine percent of TRIO students return for a second semester as compared to 40% without TRIO. TRIO is working, and it is transforming lives.

Gretchen Loase teaches and tutors for TRIO. She has established a warm TRIO center that empowers students academically. TRIO was recently renewed at Westchester Community College for several more years, so things are not uniformly hopeless.

Dr. Hankin lamented that Head Start, a powerful and highly effective early childhood educational intervention for economically disadvantaged students, was phased out. Dr. Hankin counsels that learning must start in the home. It is imperative that parents of economically disadvantaged students read to their children. If this is not feasible, parents should seek help through after school programs to help their children with reading and math. Dr. Hankin's insight is precisely the rationale for the model program that my math partner Melvin Butts has innovated at Redeemer Church in the Bronx. His after school tutorial program provides help to hundreds of underserved young people in areas such as Math, Science, and SAT preparation. Pockets of excellence to serve as models for the sigfluence generation do exist. However, there are not nearly enough.

Dr. Hankin is an optimist, but he is not sanguine that America can become #1 in the rate of college graduation by 2020. He laments, "We have lost our way." More students are dropping out. A turnaround in education cannot be accomplished by President Obama alone.

I asked Dr. Hankin whether his effective leadership was an outgrowth of a "servant leader" philosophy, a philosophy in which the role of the leader is to provide the necessary resources for growth to those under your responsibility. Dr. Hankin agreed. His current vision even includes the continuous education of Baby Boomers, who need all the help that they can get to partner a sigfluence generation with the youth of today.

Riverside High School

During the spring of 2010, I despaired at the lack of follow-up by principals from Harlem, Yonkers, Mt. Vernon, and Queens. Professor Melvin Butts and I had delivered five, ninety minute College Success Seminars to over 1,000 economically disadvantaged students. Our message, to pursue academic excellence and take only rigorous high school courses, was enthusiastically praised by over 99% of the students in their evaluations. Unfortunately, not a single principal scheduled us for a seminar for the 2011-2012 school year.

I asked one principal if we could innovate my College Statistics course at his high school. Sadly, he did not return my phone calls or emails. As I researched this book, I found that I was not alone. There is a chasm between secondary education and college. High schools believe that their responsibility is merely to get the students to graduate. At the same time, colleges flunk out over 80% of students who require three or more remedial classes in college, and they blame high schools for poor preparation.

No party feels responsible for the sigfluence of continuous caring for the student K-16. The exception was Riverside High School in Yonkers. Our glorious success at Riverside High School was due to the interesting combination of mud on the Croton Aqueduct trail, the continuous partnership of Professor Melvin Butts and our serendipitous connection with Principal Steven Murphy, Assistant Principal Carol Baiocco, and Master Teacher Maria Rodriguez. The mud on the bike trail forced me onto the streets of Yonkers, where I chanced upon this marvelous school. Steve and Carol enthusiastically supported our College Success seminar and the subsequent innovating of College Statistics at Riverside High School. We raised money for college tuition and books for the initial class of nine. We achieved 100% success, with a median or middle score of B+/A-. The students loved the course, the teachers loved the course, and the administration of both the high school and Concordia College loved the course. We plan to reach fifty students next year at Riverside High School with the same course.

President Obama, please understand that our over the top success dramatically helped one or two students significantly improve their chances of obtaining a college degree, but we still have one or two million economically disadvantaged to reach. And it took Professor Butts and me three years to find one venue to reach one or two students.

President Obama, will you please stop making statements that give people the false hope that we can reach #1 in the world in college graduation rates? More importantly, please read about Superintendent Pierorazio's beautiful educational innovations that could help thousands of students. Pierorazio's program, along with countless others, currently lies in limbo as a result of budget cuts. Just as a good marriage requires two engaged partners, productive relationships of any nature require honesty, a willingness to face reality, and the resolve to maintain rewarding mutual benefit. Political lies, like America can become #1 in college graduation rates, are only possible through our complicity. America wants to live in a constant state of deep denial. The Sigfluence Generation, our 18-25 year olds, has the potential to change this.

How We Fool Ourselves

Great literature and film frequently provide us with a much needed perspective. Moby Dick, one of the great novels of all time, features a madman, Ahab, who brings destruction to nearly his entire crew. Like us, his men are mesmerized by his confidence, charisma, and competence – the three C's. Nearly every person on board buys into Ahab's blind, obsessive pursuit of the white whale. As a manual on how to seize the collective consciousness of a nation Moby Dick holds its own. Carl Jung counseled us to develop ourselves. The best thing we can do for ourselves is nurture our own talents before we attempt to serve others. (For more insights into Jung's impressive canon of work, start with *Man and His Symbols*.) Penetrating Jung's depths is a lifelong pursuit and a worthy one.

Contrary to scientific evidence, many still believe that global warming is just a myth. Global warming is just one of many" Inconvenient Truth's" that our society clings to. We ignore inconvenient truths because denial is more comforting. Stanford University psychologist Leon Festinger wrote the following:

"A man with a conviction is a hard man to change.
Tell him you disagree and he turns away. Show
him facts or figures and he questions your sources.
Appeal to logic and he fails to see your point."[6]

Dr. Festinger aptly captures our propensity for denial.
We were #1 in education decades ago. President Obama
wants us to believe that our country can become #1 in
college graduation rates by 2020, and we want to believe
him. His message is much more comforting than mine.
My message is that we are a nation in denial. Our neglect
of the economically disadvantaged in education stands in
stark opposition to two of the pillars of American society,
equal opportunity and progress. The sigfluence generation
has to usher in an era of connection and concern. Our
crumbling educational system is a reflection of our
crumbling interior lives. Schools are a reflection of society
and society is us. After three years of Sisyphean struggle,
our Riverside High School innovation may have
significantly helped one or two people. If one or two million
people commit to ameliorating our problems in education,
we might not become #1 in the world, but we surely will
have made great progress.

LIE #2 – The Purpose Of American Education Is To Educate

Why Do We Have to Learn This Stuff?

Forty-three years ago, I started teaching at Hawthorne Junior High School. Thank God I was athletic, because I broke up a fight almost every day. The school was sheer bedlam. I was an above average first year teacher. I did not quit at noon on day one, like one of my freshman colleagues, and I was actually able to teach because I was strict and had discipline. Mary, a student in both Miss D's class and mine, told me one day,

"Mr. Loase, you are mean. Why can't you be like Miss D? She's nice." I asked Mary, "What do you mean by mean?" She answered, "All we do in your class is work. We can't talk. We can't chew gum. All we do is work." I continued, "Miss D is nice. What do you mean by nice?"Mary responded, "We can talk in Miss D's. We threw spitballs the first week." Then Mary stood tall, palpably brightened and revealed, "And yesterday we threw a desk out of Miss D's window. That was fun."

It was easy to consider inner city teaching as theater of the absurd - Three Penny Opera in reality. To make matters worse, the curriculum was insane. I was supposed to teach the New Math, invented by brilliant and clueless mathematicians, to a bunch of young people who could barely do fractions.

This question is for you. Given the axioms of the real number system, prove that a negative times a negative is a positive. Take 5 minutes. Do not peek.

Answer
Axiom 1) Start with basic knowledge of addition of integers. For example:

$$2 \times (+3) = +3 + (+3) = +6$$

2 x (-3) = -3 + (-3) = -6
This addition property of the integers is considered axiomatic.
Axiom 2) (-3) x 2 = 2 x (-3) = -3 + (-3) = -6
Commutative Law of Multiplication
Axiom 3) a x 0 = 0
Axiom of multiplication of any real number by 0 = 0
Axiom 4) a + -a = 0
Additive Inverse Property of Integers
Axiom 5) a (b + -b) = a (0) = 0
Follows from Axioms 3 and 4
Axiom 6) a (b + c) = a x b + a x c
Distributive Property
Now we are ready to prove why a negative integer times a negative integer is positive.

Proof
Example – We learn best through example.
1)   -2 x (5 + -5) = (-2) x 0 = 0
Axioms 3 and 4. Did you already forget?
2)   (-2) x (5 + -5) = (-2) x 5 + (-2) x (=5)
Axiom 6 – Distributive Property
3)   (-2) x 5 = 5 (-2) = -2 + -2 + -2 + -2 + -2 = -10
Axioms 1 and 2
4)   (-2) x 5 + (-2) (-5) = -10 + (-2)(-5) = 0
Did you forget #1 above?
5)   Let x = (-2)(-5)
      -10 + x = 0
      Substitution Axiom
6)   -10 + x = 0
Add 10 to both sides of the equation-one of Euclid's basic axioms. If you do not remember it, do not feel bad. You are an American. We revel in mathematical ignorance, but you are 2400 years behind Euclid.
7)   (-10 + x) + 10 = 0 + 10
8)   0 + 10 = 10
Identity for Addition Axiom
9)   (-10 + x) + 10 = -10 + (x + 10)
Associative Law Axiom
10)   -10 + (x + 10) = -10 + (10 + x)
Associative Law Axiom. Did you already forget?

11) $-10 + (10 + x) = (-10 + 10) + x$
Did you forget Associative Law Axiom again?
12) $(-10 + 10) = 0$
Did you forget Axiom 4?
13) $0 + x = x$
I am losing patience.
14) $x = \text{answer} = 10$

⅄   If you are uncomfortable with the New Math, imagine teaching this to 180 economically disadvantaged 8th graders. By my second week, I had thrown out this lunatic curriculum and was teaching fractions, decimals and percentages, only to find out that most of my students did not even know the times table. Yet the American public believes that it knows the solution to all of our educational problems. Trust me, neither you nor I have all the answers. Furthermore, one has to question whether the purpose of education at Hawthorne Junior High School was to educate or create an insurmountable barrier to perpetuate economic disadvantage.

Numerous studies have shown that there is a clear connection between unequal educational opportunities and housing policies, and Yonkers was no exception. For decades, a racist housing policy had engendered a segregated school system that featured separate and extremely unequal resources for the west side poor. Yonkers lost virtually every racial discrimination lawsuit brought by the NAACP, the Justice Department, along with numerous others. Yonkers in the late 1960s and 1970s was overtly racist. (The 180 economically disadvantaged students that I taught had to share 20 books, while each of the middle class students on the east side of Yonkers had a book for home and a separate book for their school locker. Today, things are better in Yonkers education, but the cuts, that Superintendent Pierorazio was forced to make, threaten to decimate his impressive set of educational innovations.)

Although the shape of education has changed during the past forty years, the poor continue to inherit the same educational disadvantage my students encountered four decades ago. We have to overcome our denial and level the educational playing field in America. We have to listen to the exemplars from this book and alter course. America has to scrutinize our failing educational system and creatively innovate ways for the poor to achieve success in education. We have to move beyond mere access and strive for success. We have to explore credentialing and the covert bias inherent in our professional societies, like entrance criteria that lack proof of validity. Why was I required to take 8 semesters of Calculus to teach the times table? What is the relationship between what we are required to take in college and what we use professionally? Let us return to prehistoric times for some perspective.

A Brief History of the World of Work

Our current system of categorizing people for positions at work dates to Neanderthal times. What might the world of work looked like back then? Jean Auel's *The Clan of the Cave Bear* may shed light on the role of the esteemed hunters:

"The land was unbelievably rich, and man only an insignificant fraction of the multifarious life that lived and died in that old, ancient Eden. ...The capable experienced hunters of the clan were as skilled in defense as they were in offense, and when the safety or security of the clan was threatened or if they wanted a warm winter coat decorated by nature, they stalked the unsuspecting stalker."[7]

The life and death of the clan depended upon the effectiveness of the hunter. This position (presumably one of high status) was likely awarded on the basis of pure competence. Otherwise, the group would be vulnerable to attack, lack an adequate food supply, languish, and die. There were no Harvard business schools, Stanford law degrees, or University of California – Berkeley engineering programs to ensure lives of privilege and comfort. The world of work has grown incredibly complex, problematic, and less fair than it was in Neanderthal times. Could you imagine what prehistoric hunting school would have been like in today's terms?

The applicants for hunting school would naturally outnumber the positions, therefore we would have to winnow the job seekers sensibly. Since a hunter was of the same status (in Neanderthal terms) as a Congressional Representative, professor, doctor, or lawyer, we would have to establish screening procedures. Stone Age arithmetic would be part of the program for the prospective hunter along with some type of language skill test. Some members of the clan would be particularly skilled in Stone Age arithmetic and Neanderthal language, therefore the parents of prospective hunters would seek them out to hone the skills of their progeny. They might even give the teachers an extra share of smoked salmon or bear fur in order to guarantee that their children obtained the coveted position of hunter. Obviously, competence in Stone Age arithmetic and Neanderthal language have nothing to do with hunting proficiency and consequently, the tribe would likely die. Let us examine a more recent situation in the world of work.

The twentieth century witnessed profound changes in the labor force, including women's participation and activism, the civil rights movement, the expansion of unions, current challenges of globalization, international competition, a peripatetic and overworked labor force, and the denial and neglect of sigfluence in its essential link to job satisfaction.

Many myths perpetuate the job status quo in America. The Sigfluence Generation should consider each myth, the opposite of each, and find truth somewhere in between.

The myths that the Sigfluence Generation need to examine involve professional training, consumer protection, an idealized view of teachers' influence, the importance of a high status job, and the American tendency to over-identify with our job.

We lie to ourselves about professional training. I certainly did not need 8 semesters of calculus to teach the times table and break up fights on a regular basis at Hawthorne Junior High School. However, in order to chair Concordia College's math department, I needed all my 100 credits past Calculus and my doctoral training. We need to honor the Liberal Arts, and resist reducing college to a trade school, but we need to explore how certain college requirements repeatedly lead to failure.

My master's degree in Counseling Psychology dispensed a plethora of information that was quickly forgotten. My practical courses on how to counsel were invaluable, but 90% of my training to become a guidance counselor was dubious. And I became the President of the Association for Measurement and Evaluation of Counseling for New York State.

Do Professional Schools Train or Ration Jobs?

We cannot continue the charade that all professional training is essential to job performance. Christopher Jencks challenged the validity of professional credentials decades ago in the following:

> "Neither tests nor diplomas are likely to correlate very well with job performance, although there will be some exceptions. We doubt that the present court will pursue this logic to its revolutionary conclusion. Nonetheless some (challenges to the system of tests and Credentials) are likely to be successful."[8]

Dr. Jencks wrote this forty years ago, when the poor had a chance in the courts of America. Forty years ago the Supreme Court (1971 Griggs versus Duke Power Company) ruled that the tests that business used for promotion had to be validated. The burden of proof to show a connection between the test and eventual job performance rested with the employer.

My mentor at Columbia University, the late Dr. Richard Wolf, gave me a copy of the Griggs Decision. Dr. Wolf said: "It reads like great literature," and it did.

The Supreme Court expressed American ideals of fairness in the following:

> "If an employment practice cannot be shown to be related to job performance, the practice is prohibited... neither the high school completion requirement nor the general intelligence test is

shown to bear a demonstrable relationship to successful performance of the job."[9]

The Supreme Court of 2011 is unlikely to "pursue this logic to its revolutionary conclusion." The Court is supremely in favor of business and against fairness toward the individual. It is not radical to insist on fairness. It is not radical to re-engineer our society, so that people can prepare for certain jobs without years of professional training, which does a better job of rationing jobs than imparting essential skills. The Sigfluence Generation has to enter politics, shape politics, and insist on a return to fairness and the spirit of the Griggs' Decision.

Justice Clarence Thomas presided over the Equal Opportunity Commission in the mid 90s. Mr. Thomas was ostensibly responsible for upholding the rights of people who were the victims of discrimination. Mr. Thomas reduced the number of job discrimination cases to a trickle. In 1989 the Ward Coves Supreme Court decision shifted the burden of proof of unfairness to the employee. We had lost the poetic idealism of Griggs. Mr. Thomas was the wolf guarding the chickens, and his protection of big business did not go unnoticed. He was rewarded with a Supreme Court Justice seat, and my idealism and hope for a fairer America was shattered.

During the Senate confirmation hearings, I was taking a post doctoral course interpreting the Rorschach (ink blot test). Our class spent the first 30 minutes of every session discussing the ease with which Clarence Thomas was able to deceive the panel. He claimed that he was the "victim of a high tech lynching," and he was outraged by the personal attacks given his "46 years of public service." At the time he was 46.

The Sigfluence Generation has to uncover our lies, confront illusion and deception, and create a more caring, sharing nation. It may take decades. Justices Roberts, Thomas and the conservative block will continue to dominate the Court for years to come, but we can evolve into a more enlightened nation. Fifty years ago, it was unimaginable to elect a Black President. Hopefully, fifty years from now we will have faced our denial and remedied the societal suffering that is the consequence of our heretofore unchallenged lies.

Top Colleges Largely for the Elite

David Leonhardt recently wrote an article linking elite colleges and elite jobs. All nine of the Supreme Court Justices attended elite colleges, as did the last four Presidents of the United States. America has institutionalized Ivy League credentials as sine qua non for top jobs. Given the fact that these colleges are frightfully expensive, it is not surprising that only the very wealthy have the resources to spend in excess of $250,000.00 on a college education.

Some efforts have been made to open Ivy doors to economically disadvantaged students. Harvard recently guaranteed four years of tuition and room and board to qualified students who were economically disadvantaged. Most of the other Ivy League schools have followed suit. Though this is progress, educational opportunities are still weighed heavily in favor of the wealthy. In 2010 at the country's most selective 193 colleges, only 15% of the entering freshmen came from the bottom half of the income distribution, while sixty-seven percent came from the highest quarter. President Marx of Amherst expressed the problem perfectly when he stated that:

> "We claim to be part of the American dream and of a system based on merit and opportunity and talent....yet we are actually part of the problem of the growing economic divide rather than part of the solution."

One of the factors which led to the increased support for economically disadvantaged students from Harvard was research done by former Princeton President William Bowen. Mr. Bowen found that top colleges did not give an admissions advantage to economically disadvantaged students, despite claims to the contrary.

In an attempt to remedy this, President Marx launched an effort at Amherst to increase the enrollment of talented, economically disadvantaged students by emphasizing financial aid, focusing on attracting qualified community college transfers, and recognizing that SAT scores might be unreliable predictors of college success, particularly for students coming from Savage Inequality high schools. Today, thanks to the leadership of President Marx, Amherst has a higher percentage of low-income students than nearly any other elite college in the country.

President Marx has shown us that we can transform American college education, one college at a time. Mr. Leonhardt said it perfectly when he wrote:

> "the (Amherst) model isn't only the fairest one and the right one for the economy. It's also the best for the colleges themselves. Attracting the best of the best - not just the best of the affluent - and letting them learn from one another is the whole point of a place like Amherst."[10]

What Do You Really Learn in College?

I feel lucky that Manhattan College had such high standards. I was required to take thirty advanced math credits beyond Elementary Calculus. After three semesters of Calculus, my peers and I took a course called Linear Algebra. It was tough. My friend Rich had earned A's in calculus 1, 2 and 3, but Linear Algebra was so tough for him that he switched majors from math to business. I do not feel sorry for him. He is probably doing very well in business, earning a lot more than a college professor. However, as my story about Rich shows, college has a lot of collateral damage. Too often, students are screened out of college randomly and arbitrarily. If Rich had taken the Linear Algebra course that I now teach, he would have gotten an easy A. I am a very well prepared and clear teacher, and I give easy tests. Manhattan College robbed the world of a possible math teacher in Rich, but provided me with the foundation to earn a doctorate in math and psychology, which has opened wonderful avenues for me. The same high standards, that empowered me, killed Rich's math career.

Richard Arum and his colleague in research, Josipa Roksa, spent four years following several thousand college students at more than two dozen, two and four year colleges and universities. They found that many students showed little if any significant progress in critical thinking, complex reasoning, and writing throughout their entire four years of college. In addition, Dr. Arum and Dr. Roksa found that a large numbers of students were making their way through college with little exposure to academic rigor, modest effort, and no meaningful improvement in writing and reasoning.[11]

If so many students invest so little time in study, demonstrate negligible gains in academic skills, and then graduate college, I rest my case. The major purpose of college is not to educate but to perpetuate privilege, maintain an equilibrium between employment supply and demand, provide an enviable environment for professors' research, and serve the whims of professional societies. When there were too many students majoring in Computer Science years ago, the Association for Computer Machinery (the professional association of Computer Science professionals) raised the level of advanced math for a computer science degree. This was great for me, since I teach advanced math, but how we treat the weak is a reflection of our national character. Our nation, professional societies, and colleges are perpetuating a cycle of incarceration and poverty for a large segment of the population due to unchallenged, covertly biased educational credentials. The Sigfluence Generation has to transform our system of higher education. There are vested interests within our colleges and professional societies that will resist any call for transformation, and the current Supreme Court offers little hope of ushering in a spirit of enhanced fairness and validity in professional training. But let us be patient. It took 60 years for America to progress from the Atlanta race riots and Rosa Parks to the election of Barack Obama. Over the next 60 years, college could transform itself into the beacon of hope and opportunity that is currently an elusive ideal.

LIE #3 - There Exist Omniscient Supervisors Who Can Validly And Reliably Evaluate And Rank Teachers

During my forty two years in education, I have been evaluated over thirty times. Overall, things have gone well. I have been a clear and well prepared teacher and professor, but I always anxiously awaited my supervisor's evaluation. Fortunately, I have taught in environments that suited me, and I have never had a problem with my evaluations.

With that said, teacher evaluations are a lot less useful than we would like to believe. Supervisors are too busy dealing with their own problems, which in Yonkers included budget cuts, violence, lawsuits, angry parents, problems ad nauseam. There are some teachers who are so incompetent that their teaching simply cannot be rectified. For the 5% that this applies to, it is necessary for a supervisor to gracefully lead them out of education. The rest of us however, possess a wide range of talents, strengths, and weaknesses, and what some administrators may view as a weakness, others might consider a strength. Let me illustrate.

After my second year in teaching, it became obvious to me that my students were entering 8th grade math with third grade skills at best. Therefore, I approached the new principal with a novel idea. I would recruit education majors from Manhattan College and Mt. St. Vincent to tutor the 100 students who had been left behind. I would be responsible for these students and offer them early promotion to their next grade, if they attended class regularly and passed each major subject. I trained the college students on Saturdays, roughly thirty each year. The results were magical. Eighty percent of the repeat participants passed all their subjects and were promoted early to the next grade. I felt like the Pied Piper, joyfully witnessing the innovation of a model program that transformed the education of students who were typically required to repeat grades. Responsibility Training was such a success that it was highlighted by the American School Board Journal as a national model for inner city innovation. Sometime during the third year of the program, I switched into the role of guidance counselor. Soon thereafter, Yonkers laid off hundreds of teachers. I too was laid off and my model program, Responsibility Training, was ended. Thereafter, I spent one year teaching math at Horace Mann - one of America's elite, private high schools. After a year, I was called back to Yonkers and was given the choice between returning to my old school or starting fresh at Saunders High School. There was a new principal at Hawthorne and she interviewed me for my old job. During the interview, I asked her whether or not she supported Responsibility Training. She said, "John, if a kid gets let back, they get left back." Responsibility Training was a national model, and the pride of my former principal, but the new principal had no support for the program. One principal rated my work as an over the top success - a national model, while the other considered the entire enterprise a failure. This is one of the many reasons for tenure in education. One principal might evaluate a teacher with outstanding ratings, while another principal may have an entirely different perspective.

Throughout my college teaching career, I have received both state and national teaching awards. I am very grateful to President Joseph Hankin (Westchester Community College) and my mentor Louis Rotando for valuing my work. Some college presidents would not approve of my books on sigfluence. They also might feel that I am not failing a sufficient number of students to ensure high levels of rigor in my college classes. Evaluation of teachers and professors is a highly subjective process, but we humans refuse to acknowledge the arbitrariness and poor reliability of professional evaluation.

We Need Approval

There are certain core needs that drive our acceptance of an omniscient supervisor. One of the most basic is the need for approval. Maslow's hierarchy of human needs starts with food and shelter, but quickly moves into emotional needs with self-actualization at the top. But before we get to self-actualization, we need to develop secure relations within our environment.

Please read the important work by Erik Erikson, *Life Cycle Completed.* Dr. Erikson spent years interviewing people about their life stages. The struggle in our earliest years between trust and mistrust is basic to our development. We need to be loved in order to love. Our core need for love is mirrored in our need for approval by our supervisors. Administrators do not observe teachers or professors very often. Since I earned the highest rank of Full Professor fifteen years ago, I have been observed twice.

According to our absurd educational paradigm beginning teachers get observed two or three times, and their annual teaching evaluation is based on the subjective impression of the evaluator. Due to America's obsession with testing we judge teachers on the basis of a few actual observations coupled with student performance on tests. This reliance on statistical measures to evaluate teachers, assistant principals, principals, superintendents, and school systems fills another basic human need, the need for certainty.

Certainty

I ask my College Statistics class to complete this sentence:
The higher your level of education, the _____ your certainty.
Almost everyone says higher. The correct answer is lower. The more you know, the more you challenge certainty. Certainty is comforting, but certainty is founded on ignorance.

In recent years universities have researched Certainty Beliefs. The Max Planck Institute for Human Development explored the relationship between students' level of certainty of knowledge and school achievement. They found that the higher the level of certainty, the lower the students' school achievement. Despite this finding, the field of certainty research has not achieved a consensus on many of the central questions in this new field.[12]

Over 60 years ago, Bertrand Russell wrote brilliantly about certainty as a vice in the following:

"The demand for certainty is one that is natural to man, but is nevertheless an intellectual vice... (Certainty)....is demanded of those who undertake to lead populations with slogans like - kill the Croats and let the Serbs reign. Exterminate the Jews and everyone will be virtuous. To endure uncertainty is difficult, but so are most of the other virtues."[13]

Dr. Russell is so right. Enduring uncertainty is difficult for us. However, it is wiser to develop ourselves than to rely upon the certainty of others. Certainty kills. Hitler, Mussolini and Mao preached certainty. Dr. Russell preaches uncertainty. Uncertainty would have led to a better 20th century.

Some look to mathematics for certainty. I did in my early twenties. Then, I discovered possible contradictions in mathematics at the elementary level that shook the foundation of mathematics in the early 20th century. Even if we ignore the foundational problems in mathematics and pretend that the Calculus is perfect and certain, we still have a problem. Statistics is based on Calculus. When we use statistics we replace the 100% certainty of Calculus with levels of confidence in Statistics. There is no such thing as 100% confidence in Statistics. We usually settle for 95% confidence in the effectiveness of our prescription drugs, validity of new research results, and acceptance of new ideas. Not only is certainty replaced by confidence, but many educational decisions are made without the proper use or understanding of Statistics. Let me explain.

Years ago, my wife taught in a Savage Inequality school in the Bronx. Joe, a gifted principal, was leading the school in what appeared to be a positive direction. Things were bad, and most of the students scored below the state norms on the all or nothing state competence measures. One day, Joe told me that the school was closing, despite the clear statistically significant gains made by the students on the state test. Closing the school meant that Joe would be gone, most of the experienced teachers would be replaced with raw beginners, and chaos would ensue. I told Joe that I would give his school free consulting, demonstrate that the gains that he had led were real and impressive, and that the school should not close. Joe thanked me but ignored my free consulting. I would have testified to the parents, the local Board of Education, and the Superintendent that the school should stay open. It closed, and just as suspected a new principal with inexperienced teachers took over. Sadly, it takes many years of hard work to become an effective teacher. Joe's school quickly became a dangerous place to learn or teach. My wife left the school shortly after a boy was nearly killed during a savage fight that might have been avoided had things not deteriorated so dramatically. The new school may have looked good on paper, but many students and teachers suffered from the politically expedient decision to close the school.

At the core of the decision to close the school was the lie that omniscient administrators can create tests that effectively evaluate schools. Also at the core of the decision was a lack of basic statistical literacy. As a nation we are ignorant of basic statistical literacy. We are losing business competitiveness due to our inability to produce more engineers and mathematicians. This represents the elite level of mathematics. My counsel to Joe was based on Statistics 101, the lowest level of mathematics. Sadly, my advice went over the heads of Joe and the other educational leaders, who ordered the schools' closing.

At the heart of our emphasis on testing in education is our need for certainty. I am an expert on testing. Visit my website sigfluence.com. Download my free book – *The Sigfluence Generation*. The book, and the Sigfluence Survey that served as the foundation for the book, took 27 years to develop. Most education tests do not have any evidence that confirms their reliability or validity. The public wants there to be an omniscient Superintendent or Commissioner of Education that can develop the perfect tests to perfectly evaluate student progress, to perfectly evaluate teacher performance, and to serve as the basis for perfect teacher rankings.

One unintended consequence of this desire for certainty is the creation of environments that are particularly conducive to deceit and cheating. In Georgia, Governor

Nathan Deal revealed widespread cheating in the Atlanta public schools. At least 44 schools and 178 teachers and principals were involved in a conspiracy of silence, which eventually led back to the Superintendent of Schools, Dr. Beverly Hall. In 2009, Dr. Hall had been named the National Superintendent of the Year, exemplary test scores being the basis for her national award. Dr. Hall fed everyone's insatiable need for certainty, and in the process she poisoned a school district. We have to strike a balance between quantitative and qualitative measures. We need a new paradigm- one that fosters a partnership between teachers, administrators, and parents. The Sigfluence Generation has to transform American education.

Kafka

The older I get the more I feel like Joseph K., the respectable bank worker, who is suddenly arrested, in Kafka's *The Trial.* Joseph spends the rest of his life fighting an unknown charge against himself.

Just like Joseph K., teachers are evaluated, ranked, and made culpable for educational progress, or lack thereof, without their input or wisdom. Teachers are being evaluated by inherently limited and imperfect testing measures, and no one asks them, the leading experts on student progress, for their recommendations. We are totally ignoring the need and potential for sigfluence as sources of motivation. Education needs to be about serving students. Our need for certainty predisposes school districts to test, test, and retest, but at best a test is an imperfect snapshot of a student's educational progress. At present, we ignore the leading expert on the student's progress – the teacher.

As I reflect on our interviews with exemplary educators, my choice of experts was based upon my assessment that these people shared a servant-leader philosophy. They were in education to serve students. Each exemplar was delighted to contribute ideas to improve education. They all gave specific strategies by which we can positively transform American education. Not one exemplar suggested better testing.

Gretchen Loase highlighted the joy she experiences as a tutor in TRIO, a national model for college success of economically disadvantaged students. TRIO helps students with academic problems, financial problems, and scheduling problems. It is there to provide a consistent, caring relationship for students who otherwise would have great difficulties navigating college.

Dr. Hankin echoed Gretchen's praise of TRIO. TRIO had nearly a 90% success rate among students returning for the second semester. Dr. Hankin believed that TRIO was responsible for this success rate. Yet, TRIO is always on the educational cutting block in an attempt to reduce our national deficit. If we cut exemplary programs like TRIO, we have to plan for higher prison costs.

Sigfluence

The common denominator, of the people I interviewed from the world of education, was a servant leader model. I could not have endured the dozens (if not hundreds) of unreturned phone calls from principals, ignoring my request to deliver College Success Seminars and my College Statistics course, without the partnership of Melvin Butts. Melvin visited the superintendent of the troubled Mt. Vernon School District when it became obvious that we were getting nowhere fast. It still took another year, another Mt. Vernon High School principal, the advocacy of Gospel Choirs of Mt. Vernon, and Director Carson Stapleton to actually meet with Mt. Vernon school administrators and propose our innovations. We are still waiting to launch our work, but Professor Butts was instrumental in our perseverance. He champions the concept of "value added." Our seminar adds educational value to many students. It is worthwhile, even if only one out of 100 integrate its motivational power into improved study. Given our enthusiasm, the obvious educational need, and the power of our brutally direct presentation we should have spoken to over 10,000 students by now. But we have given "Value Added" to over a thousand.

Maria Rodriguez, my Riverside High School partner, understood the importance of our College Statistics innovation. She told me that next year, when we expand the course from nine students to two classes of twenty-five, we will have made a real impact. Ms. Rodriguez does not need an administrator rating and ranking her. She and the vast majority of teachers are motivated by sigfluence. We need to harness the Need for Sigfluence and the Potential for Sigfluence from our teachers. We trust our children, our most prized possessions, to teachers, but our overemphasis on testing betrays our lack of confidence in the wisdom of these very same teachers.

Principal Steven Murphy and Assistant Principal Carol Baiocco trusted Professor Butts and me to deliver our 90 minute College Success Seminar to the entire eleventh grade at Riverside High School. They then gave us more trust by supporting my College Statistics course innovation. The Concordia College Dean of the College, Sherry Fraser, and Dean of Faculty, Mandana Nakhai were also enthusiastically behind our outreach to economically disadvantaged students. All parties were motivated by sigfluence. There was no status in a college innovating a Statistics course in an economically disadvantaged high school. Colleges pay lip service to teaching, but some of the worst teaching goes on in large auditoriums at elite universities, where elite students are herded like cattle into lectures. Colleges prize publications and major grants. Both college and K-12 education have to transform themselves from credentialing institutions to models of service. Our current educational system is inefficient and seething with denial and illusion. Administrators, K-16, have to become partners with teachers in making a difference. Administrators need to weed out the 5% of people, who are ill suited for the teaching profession. But the vast majority of educators are motivated to make a difference. Our current lie, that tests validly and reliably rate and rank teachers, feeds the denial and delusion of the American public. Our current American educational system simply perpetuates privilege and poverty, and the ratio of poverty to privilege is rapidly increasing, threatening our current and future well-being.

America has to transform K-16 education. We need to develop continuity of caring K-16. At present there are too many places where students fall through the cracks. In some economically disadvantaged high schools, up to half of the students entering high school fail to graduate within four years. Those who do, frequently enter college remedial programs, the kiss of death. Transforming American education will take decades if we confront our current denial and delusion. Things look hopeful. Our young people are not the self-absorbed narcissists that some believe them to be. They have the potential and need to make a difference.

LIE 4 – Our 18-25 Year Olds
Are Self-Absorbed Narcissists

Melissa Hamilton-Holberg contradicted this lie in a letter to Utne Reader. She wrote:

"These same students, labeled by Utne the 'Me, Me, Me generation, spoke (at an environmental studies graduation dinner from Ithaca College) about the importance of community, friendship, respect, and of a longing to make a positive difference in the world."[14]

The Sigfluence Generation

It took me twenty-seven years of research to find what Melissa observed in one evening. Five years ago, two graduate students of mine, Teresa Osadnik and Grace Nayudupalli Dickson, spent two years in partnership with data mining expert, Dr. Piliouras, in an effort to uncover the motivations of 18-25 year olds. We analyzed 104 responses to a Marketing and Sigfluence Survey developed by Dr. Piliouras and myself. It took Teresa and Grace 18 months to enter the data. Then I spent an additional year looking for "golden nuggets" of insight into the dynamics of our young people. I relied upon the data to inspect relationships. Day one after the data was entered, I explored several thousand correlations. Correlation is one of the most important topics in Statistics. For example, the higher your level of education, the higher your salary – close to 100% correlation. This is a positive direct correlation. On the other hand, the lower your earned run average in baseball, the higher your salary, a correlation of nearly negative 100%, also a great predictor. In College Statistics, you learn that correlation does not prove causality, but confluence leads to strong insights.

Leading Findings

Of the thousands of analyses I performed, thanks to SPSS and an efficient computer, the following results stood out:

1) The best predictor of living a satisfactory life was one's Potential for Sigfluence. It is more important to wake up animated by the potential to make a difference today than to rest on your laurels from yesterday.

2) The Need for Sigfluence and Potential for Sigfluence were also highly related to life satisfaction. Here we uncover another lie. Education and psychology list helping others as an interest or value, like stamp collecting or tennis. We are lying to our students. Making a positive difference is a fundamental need of humans – a need that is widely neglected in education, as well as our personal and professional lives.

3) Women scored significantly higher than men in Potential, Need and Actual Sigfluence (the sigfluence you believe you have achieved). When transforming education, we have to educate men about their current neglect of their fundamental need to affect sigfluence. In this area, women can serve as mentors.

4) Perhaps most importantly, this sample of 542 college students scored significantly higher in Actual, Need and Potential for Sigfluence than my previous sample of 282, who represented prior generations.

Every study has limitations. My study was limited to two small private Christian colleges in Westchester County. However, Abraham Maslow once quipped that psychology might profitably err from positively biasing the sample. My three year study found that our 18-25 year olds yearn to make a positive difference in the world. The focus group that I ran with our young people echoed the sentiments of Melissa Hamilton-Holberg. Mary contributed this insight:

"Generation Y has more desire for a positive influence, but they don't participate fully. The need is there but laziness and a lack of education is keeping them back. The image is that it isn't cool to help others."

Mary has hit the nail on the head. Our 18-25 year olds need education from the Baby Boomer generation on what makes a positive difference and what does not. If we continue to deny and lie about education, our 18-25 year olds will simply perpetuate our comfortable malaise.

Rasheed said it well in our focus group:

"I agree the 90s were greedy. But since 9/11 it's not just about ourselves, but everyone else in the country. Yes, this is a positive influence generation."

9/11 is the great overriding tragedy of our American lives. It took me years to recover from the images of carnage. We can turn great tragedy into sigfluence, but until education supports positive influence as a universal need, we will continue to fall short of realizing the sigfluence potential of our 18-25 year olds.

Warren Buffet and Bill Gates came to sigfluence much later in life. Both plan to donate nearly all their wealth to philanthropy. But they know it is easier to make a million than give it away wisely. Money can easily corrupt the recipient. Our 18-25 year olds have good intentions, but they need guidance from us on how to optimize sigfluence. We have to get over our denial, admit our shortcomings, and mentor a Sigfluence Generation. Education is the foundation for societal transformation.

Dr. Hankin believes that in education we have lost our way. He believes that a transformation of education cannot be done by one individual – even President Obama. He is currently developing a program of continuous education for the Baby Boomers. Education must be a lifelong pursuit for all. Baby Boomers must be educated on how to empower 18-25 year olds to transform American education. We need partnership and new connections.

Principal Steven Murphy and Assistant Principal Carol Baiocco do not see our young people as narcissists. Mr. Murphy sees the care that his high school students show toward others. Ms. Baiocco stated that the students love the environmental programs at Riverside High School. Our young people must be educated to nurture and protect our fragile environment. They need guidance from us on how to care for our physical and social environment.

Mr. Murphy wisely noted that Riverside High School students may be so committed to others that it could hold them back. I understand this insight deeply. Even altruism and kindness have limits.

When I innovated my Responsibility Training program at Hawthorne Junior High School, William was one of the students I helped. I tutored William personally, regularly counseled him, loaned him lunch money, and allowed him to visit my apartment regularly. I treated William like family. I was also regularly missing twenty or forty dollars. One of the toughest things I ever did was confront William about the missing money. He answered, "John, if I needed money, I would ask you." A week later, William's brother saved me from myself. He cautioned me that Willliam had been stealing money from their parents. Helping others is hard work. We have to educate our Millennials as to the joy and dangers of helping others. Our young people have the Potential and Need to effect a transformation in American education. But we need to share our disappointments as well as our successes, enabling the Sigfluence Generation to build on success, while avoiding some of the pitfalls created by unrestrained helping.

Two movies that I recommend to all my college students are Ikiru and Viridiana. One of my fellow teachers at Hawthorne Junior High School recommended that I view Ikiru. Her husband had been the editor of a prestigious New York magazine. Shortly after viewing Ikiru, he quit his high status job, and went looking for a job with higher Potential for Sigfluence. Our young people have to hear about the sigfluence or lack thereof that we have achieved professionally. Otherwise we perpetuate the status quo. They have to be mentored by us in order to transform American education.

Viridiana is a classic film by director Luis Bunuel. Sister Viridiana tried to help the beggars, thieves, and underclass of a city, before she was adequately developed and prepared for such a mission. She suffered grave consequences because of her premature and unreflective helping. Our young people have to be counseled to help others and simultaneously protected from the dangers and abuses of unfettered idealism.

Helping is a science (in its infancy) and an art. It is essential that our 18-25 year olds embrace helping as a universal motivation. We all need continuous education as a foundation for optimizing one's Potential for Sigfluence and personal development. Carl Jung counsels us all to improve the world by improving ourselves. One of the most important ways that millennials can fulfill their zeal for positive influence is by patiently and deliberately improving themselves.

LIE 5 - To Raise College Graduation Rates, We Must Lower Standards

When I was in my 20's, I believed in high standards. My ninth grade algebra teacher and future mentor and department chair, Louis Rotando, had high standards. Earning a 100% on his Algebra final was my motivation to become a math teacher and professor.

At Manhattan College I was required to complete nine semesters of Calculus, including two semesters of advanced engineering mathematics. I never complained. I enjoyed math and realized that math was my ticket to success. However, there were academic casualties due to the high standards. Nearly all the students taking the Intermediate Calculus class failed. Fortunately, I dropped this class and repeated Calculus I, but an entire class of future engineers and math professionals was lost due to what could only have been poor teaching.

At Hawthorne Junior High, I was expected to teach the rigorous and abstract New Math. Never trust mathematicians to devise a curriculum for the masses. For the students at elite private schools like Horace Mann and Boston Latin, the New Math was a great idea. At Hawthorne Junior High however, the New Math was absurd. I quickly adjusted and taught fractions, decimals, percent, and ultimately the times table. I was overqualified to teach Hawthorne Junior High School math by the time I graduated high school, let alone college. America loses a lot of math professionals due to unexamined college standards.

My doctoral dissertation for Columbia University Teachers College explored the relationship between the math that actuaries (applied mathematicians who usually work for insurance companies) and computer science professionals take in college and the math that they actually use on the job. Surprisingly, I found that there was a huge chasm between math taken and math used. One remarkable and puzzling finding for early career computer science professionals in particular was that the more math courses that they took in college, the less math they used on the job.

My findings were presented to the Association for Computer Machinery, a computer science society, in a lecture in which I revealed what I called the "covert bias" of their credentialing, the fact that there was no apparent validity to their required training. I suggested that a chess tournament might be just as useful as their current procedure for evaluating talent as chess might be a way for the bright, economically disadvantaged to overcome the artificial barriers erected by the ACM.

The computer science professionals were amused by my talk, however my intention was not to amuse. Not long after this lecture, my invitation to deliver a similar lecture at the Society of Actuaries, highlighting the "covert bias" within their profession, was rescinded. One of the actuarial society officers must have heard that my talk would offend the delicate sensibilities of the professional Actuary, one of the most highly paid and comfortable professionals in the world. A recent Wall Street Journal study found Actuary as one of the most desirable jobs in America. It is highly desirable when your boss does not understand the mathematics you are using to solve business issues, even if the math is not as esoteric as one would expect.

Throughout college and even into the early stages of my career, I never had a liberal or conservative bias. However, my doctoral training and dissertation coupled with my teaching experience at Hawthorne Junior High School produced my focus on fairness. There is nothing wrong with high professional standards, as long as there is a sensible and valid connection to professional practice, which is currently lacking in America. It is time to explore how to better connect person and job. Our society relies on face validity and appearance. It is time to scrutinize how we lose people, particularly the economically disadvantaged, due to untested and unchallenged face valid standards. We lose a lot of students in our high schools. Then college loses over 80% of students, who require remediation, remediation for skills that are not contributing to a better society.

Math - The Insurmountable Barrier

My first jobs at the collegiate level were adjunct counselor, math professor and consultant at CUNY - Baruch. I taught talented, economically disadvantaged students enrolled in HEOP - Higher Education Opportunity Program. After serving one semester as a college counselor, I was asked to serve as a consultant to devise a math course that would lower the high failure rate in Baruch's advanced course Financial Mathematics, which was required of all students.

After I had completed the proposal for the new course, I had to have it approved by a committee of faculty. For ninety minutes, all I heard were complaints about my proposal. To my surprise, my proposal passed. Afterwards, I visited the dean who had requested my consulting and asked, "How do you put up with this faculty?" His response was, "John, I am returning to the classroom. I have had it."

A year later, while I was teaching at my first full time position at Westchester Community College, I came across an article in The Chronicle of Higher Education which stated that Baruch was facing the possible loss of accreditation. One of the reasons given was the high failure rate of economically disadvantaged students. I have no doubt that math was a substantial roadblock to success for the gifted minority students at Baruch.

Sadly, little has changed in the past thirty years. In 2005, the United States Department of Education stated that the major obstacle to college graduation in the United States was math. They went on to say that for economically disadvantaged students, math posed an "insurmountable barrier to college graduation." Some readers may believe that present college math requirements are necessary and fair, so indulge me. Take an abbreviated quiz from remedial college algebra. Answer these two questions. You have ten minutes. Ready. Begin.

Reader Short Algebra Quiz

    1. John is jogging at 5 mph. He leaves his house at
10 AM. His wife bicycles the same path as John at
6 mph. She leaves at noon. When will John's wife
catch up with her husband?

    2. Simplify
$[(-2)^4 - 6 - 4^2] \div (-1-1)^2$

    Please check your answers.
1. X=12hrs or midnight.
2. -3/2.

These questions are similar to problems that remedial
math students have to master before enrolling in regular
college mathematics. We are killing millions of otherwise
capable college students, who simply cannot develop a
facility with Algebra. Such students inherit economic
disadvantage from their parents and their schools
institutionalize disadvantage, but our society denies that
covert bias is present in American education.
    Economically disadvantaged students usually end up in
remedial courses in college where it may take years for
them to pass College Arithmetic (a euphemism for
elementary school math) and Remedial Algebra. Over 80%
of college students who require three or more remedial
college classes do not earn a bachelor's degree within eight
years. Have you ever used any of the Algebra you just were
tested on? I loved math and feel comfortable with the very
advanced levels. However, our treatment of the weak
disadvantaged is a reflection of our national character.
American colleges and universities have failed to adjust
their curriculum to fit the joint needs of the economically
disadvantaged and society as a whole. As I pointed out
earlier, there is little relation between the math taken and
the math that is used professionally, even by the Actuary
and the computer science professional. How can we
continue to stand by the lie that we must lower standards
to raise college graduation rates? We must identify

sensible standards - standards that are fair and valid. Standards that serve both the student and society.

Math Hurts More Than the Poor

In 2007, I published an article in Focus entitled, "Statistics: A Key to Student Success in College and Life." In this article I recommended that College Statistics be required of all students, and pointed out that students could thrive in Statistics without facility in algebra. Several dozen math professors and teachers requested my free 92 page book (*Essentials of Statistics - TI83 Calculator Based*). The feedback that I received from everyone who wrote or called was 100% positive. Not one single math professional accused me of lowering standards.

There was one letter and phone call in particular that stood out. Dr. X wrote about how useful my approach would be at state university Y where he taught. Over 50% of the well qualified students never graduated. A sequence of calls from the state Governor to the College President to the Provost of the Deans to the Department Chairs revealed the source of the problem - College Algebra. The math chair revealed a persistent 50+% failure rate in College Algebra, a useless requirement of all students. In fact, Dr. X was once asked by two of his former students, a dentist and an orthopedic surgeon, why College Algebra was even required. They were very successful in their professions but had never once used College Algebra. One of the dreaded topics in College Algebra is the Simplex Method.

Simplex Method

Shortly after I started teaching College Algebra, I cut the Simplex Method from my course. I considered the topic cruel and unusual punishment. To be fair the Simplex Method is a brilliant algorithm that elite math professionals in business and myriad disciplines use to maximize profit or minimize loss.

Get Wikipedia and read the 13 page description of the Simplex Algorithm. Now imagine that you are at State

University Y. You are facile in arithmetic and algebra and you have never failed a course, but now you must learn the Simplex Method. To make matters worse, you only have a week or so to do it. It is safe to say that if you are not a math major, College Algebra will cause you a lot of heartache at the very least. It may even cost you your college degree. Yet, the requirements appear fair. No one challenges mathematicians, whose esoteric specialty terrifies all but fellow mathematicians.

Math is beautiful, logical, and vitally important. However, we would do better to motivate our Sigfluence Generation through sensible academic requirements and vital applications that dignify the college experience. We want to change the paradigm of math from the role of screening credential to the role of empowerment. Topics, like the Simplex Method, should be saved for the sole enjoyment and use of the future math professional.

Now you better understand how math prevents a large number of middle class and upper middle class students from obtaining a college degree. I shared my contempt for the Simplex Method at Math for the 21st Century, a math conference that featured seminars by national math leaders. The chair of the College Algebra Seminar was thrilled by my suggestion to abandon the Simplex Method, and asked me to write it up for national publication. In 2007 and 2009 my articles, published by Focus, called for a math transformation, in which Statistics replaces Algebra as the math requirement for every college student. Even the mathematically gifted should take Statistics and then move on to the advanced math sequence in preparation for the mathematical professions, such as math teacher/professor, mathematician, actuary, and biostatistician – all top jobs in America.

Statistics – The Solution

Math is the biggest obstacle to college graduation in the United States. Currently, Algebra is the insurmountable barrier to graduation for most remedial students. Statistics is the most valuable course an undergraduate can take according to Dr. Ben Fusaro, an esteemed founder of the Environmental Mathematics discipline in mathematics and the co-founder of the International Contest in Mathematical Modeling. When I directed the National Science Foundation program, Mathematical Modeling, my first phone call as director was to Ben. Thanks to Ben our Mathematical Modeling initiative reached a lot of American colleges and universities. We developed materials enabling advanced undergraduates to use Mathematical Modeling to solve a myriad of real-world problems. Our focus was the elite of the elite. During our partnership Ben asked me, "What is the most important undergraduate course?" Instantly I replied, "Statistics." Ben agreed. His question was rhetorical. We both knew the answer.

Statistics is inherently useful. And you can learn it with a minimum of Algebra. None of the Algebra questions you took earlier constitute an essential prerequisite for Statistics. Yet thousands of college students continue to be denied the opportunity to succeed in Statistics due to the covert bias of remedial Algebra screening them out of college.

We do not have to lower college standards. We simply have to replace covertly biased standards, like a facility in Algebra, with vital Statistics. In my 2007 Statistics article that was published in Focus, I highlighted the near 100% math success rate at Concordia College – New York, where I chair the math department. My four recommendations to colleges were:

1) Allow students in. Try to empower all college students to learn arithmetic and algebra, but allow students to take College Statistics- even if they lack facility in basic math. The calculator and a clear, compact book (like mine) can enable students to pass Statistics and earn the essential bachelor's degree.

2) Have fun. I assign *Man's Search for Meaning* by Viktor Frankl, *The Sigfluence Generation*, and *Millionaire Next Door* as required reading. Students are required to write 2 grammatically perfect short papers on the books and contribute to book

discussions, which constitutes 1/3 of their grade. English majors love this part.

3) Trim the topics. If I have not used a Statistics topic in 27 years of research and consulting, it is dropped. By pruning a course, we can emphasize topics that will be vital in the student's personal and professional life.

4) Let students use the calculator. Use of the calculator may mean that the students have not learned percentages, fractions, or other basic operations, but students have had 13 years of education before college to learn these concepts. Furthermore, we are not better teachers than public or private school educators and more importantly, we only have 15 weeks to impart the basics.

Needless to say, I was delighted when several dozen math professors and secondary math teachers responded to my 2007 Focus article with praise, appreciation, and requests for my free calculator based Statistics text. Since there are over 3000 colleges in the United States and tens of thousands of high schools, if we assume that half the educators actually used my text and followed my advice, my ideas have reached less than 1/20 of 1% of the nation. Despite my two nationally published articles calling for math transformation, 99.9% of college and secondary math departments continue to use math as a screening tool – not a gateway.

Make Math a Gateway

Derek Jeter is a superstar in baseball. Uri Treisman is a superstar in college math education. Professor Treisman performed a remarkable feat as a professor at University of California, Berkeley. Berkeley's African-American students were failing Calculus at such an alarmingly high rate that the California Bay area was losing an entire generation of Black doctors and engineers. Calculus was screening them out of their desired careers.

In an effort to figure out why this was happening, Professor Treisman decided to dorm with the students and observed their study habits. Dr. Treisman discovered that the Asian students studied together, while the African-American students studied in isolation. In order to remedy this, Professor Treisman started an African-American Honors Calculus Study Group. The students studied together and succeeded in Calculus. As a result, the Bay area has a lot more African-American doctors and engineers.

Professor Treisman now serves as a senior partner with the Carnegie Foundation. He joined Anthony S. Bryk (President of the Carnegie Foundation for the Advancement of Teaching) in writing "Make Math a Gateway, Not a Gatekeeper." This article recommends precisely what I had advocated in my 2007 article, rigorous preparation in Statistics for all students. Their reasoning behind this recommendation was that "60-70% of students placed into remedial math either do not successfully complete the sequence of required courses or avoid taking math altogether and therefore never graduate."[15]

The Carnegie Foundation has the resources to "Make Math a Gateway, Not a Gatekeeper." Professor Treisman emailed me shortly after I sent him materials related to my work. He observed that we had been working in the same vineyard. I like that metaphor. Our students have to be nurtured and cared for, just like the grapes that lead to fine wine. At Concordia College-NY, math is a gateway, not a gatekeeper, but for every gateway there are 3,000 gatekeepers

We do not have to lower our standards to better serve our students. Baby Boomers have abused their credit cards and planned poorly for retirement. A course in Statistics, that emphasized decision making related to money and meaning, could have improved their improvidence. Professor Melvin Butts, who taught at West Point, an extremely rigorous college that accepts only top of the class high school applicants, told me that the West Point ethos was to reach every student, regardless of how much tutoring or help was required. We have to replicate the West Point philosophy with our economically disadvantaged students. The widespread loss of talent, due to covertly biased standards, has to be remedied. There are more young African-American males in prison than in college. We cannot continue to simply "build more prisons." The Sigfluence Generation has to transform education.

Advanced Math

In his recent autobiography, former Federal Reserve Chairman, Alan Greenspan, revealed a deep concern for our nation's inadequate supply of math and science professionals. According to Dr. Greenspan, this neglect is a more serious threat to our nation than international terrorism.

At Concordia, I groomed one of my superstar math students for a possible Ph.D. in Mathematical Statistics at Columbia or Yale. A colleague of mine, who had earned a Ph.D. in Analysis (Advanced Calculus), mentored Ray in Calculus 5 and Real Variables (Calculus 9), two classes required by all prospective Ph.D. candidates. The chair at Columbia was delighted to have a strong American candidate for Ph.D.; every Columbia and Yale Ph.D. candidate was Asian. Ultimately, Ray decided to become a minister, but through this experience I realized that Dr. Greenspan was right. America is way behind Asia in terms of nurturing mathematical and scientific talent.

Women and minorities have been underrepresented in the mathematical sciences in the past. Exemplary programs need to be expanded to encourage talented women and minorities to pursue advanced mathematics and science in college. When I served as faculty Co-Director of a New York State Sex Equity Grant, we highlighted the wonderful math mentorship of girls K-12 in the White Plains School District. Girls were encouraged to excel in math K-12. By grade 12, nearly 50% of the advanced placement Calculus class was female. These results could easily be replicated nationwide.

At colleges like Concordia College and Hamilton College, the math departments recruit talented students with the fervor of high school football coaches pursuing athletic talent. By encouraging talented students to take advanced math, we dramatically increase their job prospects. We also address Dr. Greenspan's prescient guidance that our economic future is tied to our nurturing of mathematical and scientific talent.

We can increase college graduation rates by shifting emphasis from Algebra to Statistics for all students. We need two tracks of math for College Statistics and Calculus 1-2, and way beyond (which also includes Calculus Based Statistics). Shifting college curriculum to better serve students and society is not the same as lowering standards. In fact, we should raise expectations and standards for those with exceptional mathematical talent. Math is the key to our economic recovery and international competitiveness.

LIE 6 – Get A Good Education. Then You Get A Good Job

<u>Utopia</u>

In education utopia, inspired students are empowered by inspiring college professors. Four years later, the student leaves college, and lands a job that is financially and professionally rewarding. Decades later the polished professional retires after forty years of meaningful work. This may be possible, but it is extremely unlikely.

Instead, the typical college student enters college with the highest level of stress and the lowest level of emotional health in decades. Students are burdened by financial worries and concerns about a troubled economy. However, they maintain a high level of ambition according to a survey of 201,818 first-time full time first year students.[16]

Sadly, there are good reasons for students to be concerned. College students from economic disadvantage, who require three or more remedial classes during college, only have a 19% chance of earning a bachelor's degree within eight years.

For the fortunate 50% of students entering college, who do eventually earn a college degree, the glass is half full. However, a recent survey by the National Association of Colleges and Employers found that only 24% of 2010 college graduates who applied for a job had one upon graduation. The glass is half empty. This was up from 19% in 2009.[17] The glass is half full. Things are improving for some grads.

<u>Three College Pictures</u>

For the college remedial student, things are still dismal. The probability of graduation within four years for a student who enters college with the need of three remedial courses is roughly the same you or I replacing Derek Jeter as Yankee shortstop. That is why we hear about five year and eight year graduation rates. The four year graduation rate of American college students is so low that it is not reported very often. Obfuscation reigns supreme. Colleges cite students transferring, changing to part-time status, choosing full-time employment, and taking leaves of absence in order to hide their true graduation rate. The most reliable college graduation rate was obtained in the College Board study initiated by President Anrig. The College Board called several thousand elite college freshmen (upper 20% of their high school class) and asked them whether or not they planned to start college in September. Five years later, the students were called again. Forty percent of our elite college students had earned a four year degree within five years. This was clear – no obfuscation. Equally clear is the appalling eight year graduation rate of 19% for college remedial students. I sincerely hope that American colleges heed the advice of my 2007 article advocating Statistics as a universal college math requirement. This shift could double the college graduation rate of remedial students.

The problem with higher education in America is not initial enrollment. America provides virtually all willing students access to college. The problem is completion rates. Dr. Henry Levin of Columbia University Teachers College notes "completion rates are well below those of other countries."

Most jobs in the future will require post-secondary education. According to Anthony P. Carnevale, the Director of University of Georgetown's Center on Education and the Workforce, our dismal college completion rate will force more jobs offshore.[18] If things do not improve, we will move closer and closer to the bottom in global college graduation rates. Unemployment and underemployment will soar. A lot depends on our societal transformation of education. It will take the entire nation to transform education.

Presently, higher education is widening the gulf between the two Americas – the America of economic advantage and disadvantage. Colleges blame high schools for poor college preparation and their escalating costs of remediation. However, states and colleges have made things more difficult for low income students in recent years. Between 1995 and 2003, America's private colleges increased institutional aid by over 250% for students from families with annual incomes of more than $100,000. The increase was a paltry 50% for students from families with annual incomes of less than $20,000. Trends were very close to this disproportion in public universities as well. Universities could have cushioned low income students from the effects of rising tuition costs and decreases in state aid, but they chose not to.[19]

Exemplary programs like TRIO require consistent funding. Dr. Hankin and my wife Gretchen Loase are animated by the sigfluence of this Federal program that dramatically increases the college success rate of the economically disadvantaged. Yet, such model programs are held hostage to political sniping and short-term thinking. No one at present has responsibility or concern for a K-16 program of continuous caring and nurturing of students. We need a national infusion of sigfluence consciousness to better care for the education of our young people.

Tier 2 – College Graduates and No College Job

If only 24% of 2010 college graduates who applied for a job have one waiting after graduation, then 76% of our graduates do not have a college related job upon graduation. Of course, some grads went to law school or medical school. The MBA graduate programs prefer business students to obtain job experience before applying for a MBA, but there may not be any jobs to provide the needed experience. We are all well aware that the job market for everyone in 2011 was bleak. The only positive is that, like the housing crisis, it cannot get much worse.

In Shame, one of his many film masterpieces, Ingmar Bergman portrayed the corrosive effects of war on a loving couple, played by Max Von Sydow and Liv Ullman. It is one of the most effective anti-war movies ever made because it focuses on one couple, rather than hundreds. We feel the effects of war on a couple more easily than on hundreds of thousands of anonymous victims. Likewise, let us consider individual stories of recent college graduates and their search for any job – not a good job. Students who graduated college from 2006 – 2010 owed a median student debt of $20,000. Forty percent of our Sigfluence Generation moved back in with their parents, defeated by an impossible economy.

Dylan Suher graduated in 2010 from Washington University in St. Louis. He temporarily moved back into his parents' house. A year later and counting temporarily is starting to feel more permanent. Dylan lives with his old Little League trophies and drawers of clothes from his early childhood. Unable to obtain his dream job in publishing, his dream of having his name in lights is suspended – perhaps forever.[20]

Anna Chireno is a 2009 graduate of SUNY – Stony Brook. Her parents shuttled her off to Catholic school in Bushwick, then high school in Manhattan. She took the 7:45 AM train from a "dark, empty, urine-stained elevated platform for the No. 3 train."

It only took 30 minutes before arriving at the mosaic-tiled, less urine-stained station in lower Manhattan. Ana philosophized about what she could do with a philosophy degree from Stony Brook. Ana was transformed by Plato and W.E.R. Dubois. She reveals "where I once saw only poverty, I learned to see systemic inequality and the possibility of change."[21]

Ana couldn't be more correct. Systemic inequality is at the heart of American education, poverty, and our societal problems. As long as we continue to deny this fact and continue to elect politicians who feed our denial, we are a part of a system that perpetuates poverty and privilege. Things have gotten so bad that most college graduates are unable to get a professional start.

It is not time to abandon college or post-secondary education. College is still the best investment you can make for yourself and your children. In all likelihood, Ana and Dylan will land on their feet. Jobs will open up. America will recover from one of its sharpest economic downturns ever.

A bachelor's degree still pays off, even for jobs that don't require one, like secretaries, plumbers, and cashiers. And education seems to increase happiness and health. Dr. David Autor, an MIT economist, writes: "Sending more Americans to college is not a panacea. Not sending them to college would be a disaster."[22]

Harvard completed a study trying to determine the factors that contributed to longevity. The strongest factor was the number of years of higher education. So go for that second or third masters' degree. Even if it does not immediately get you that dream job, education is the long-term "fountain of youth."

It is hard to convey hope to people like Kyle Bishop, a 2009 graduate of the University of Pittsburgh. Kyle has spent the last two years waiting tables, delivering beer, working at a bookstore, and entering data."[23] Kyle, things will improve; things have to improve.

Before we develop Tier 3 – College Graduates Who Obtain College Related Jobs, let us spend a little time on the remedy to our currently bleak, almost tragic, job market.

Remedy

Young people have to be patient. It is not their fault that Baby Boomers have planned poorly for retirement and have to linger at their jobs longer than planned. It is not their fault that they have graduated into a job market with close to 20% unemployment and underemployment.

America should pass legislation ensuring that every 18 year old be offered a free career test, like the Strong Interest Career Test, coupled with a one hour career counseling session with a certified guidance counselor. Too many Americans fall into their careers by chance – not choice. This investment of approximately $150 ($50 for the test and $100 for the career session) could better link students with a career. Most Americans are clueless as to the thousands of career options that are available. We usually rely upon chance to obtain our jobs. Many college students would be better suited for plumbing, and many plumbers would be better suited to careers in advanced mathematics.

Note that we have not even discussed what "a good job" is. Things are so desperate that today's college graduate believes that any job is a good job. My 8th book, *The Sigfluence Generation*, reveals the high Need and Potential for Sigfluence among our 18-25 year olds. Sigfluence is very democratic. You can achieve a great deal of sigfluence in humble jobs. Inversely, you may hurt a great many people in high status jobs. Aim for sigfluence – not status.

Lower your material expectations. Smaller is better – lower taxes, lower heating expenses, and less tidying up after guests. The Mc Mansion may kill you. The ancient Pharaohs believed that the pyramids were essential to their afterlife. You will enter your afterlife prematurely by building these monster houses. No one needs 5,000 square feet of living space.

Finally, colleges and professional societies have to explore alternative routes to job preparation. Based on the reaction that I received from the National Association for Computer Machinery and the Society of Actuaries, I may not live to see this suggestion enacted, but hope springs eternal.

The 1971, the Supreme Court Griggs Decision insisted that employers had to demonstrate that employment and promotion tests were fair and valid. The late Dr. Richard Wolf, my mentor for educational and psychological measurement at Columbia University Teachers College, gave me the Griggs Decision to read. He told me it read like great literature, and it did. This sentence, which poetically reflects America's spirit and ideals, is worth repeating:

> "If an employment practice...cannot be shown to be related to job performance, the practice is prohibited."[24]

In *Ulysses*, James Joyce chronicles a day in the life of Leopold Bloom in Dublin. Bloom represents our modern day Ulysses, the hero of Homer's Odyssey. Molly Bloom, his wife, corresponds to Penelope, the faithful wife of Ulysses.

Joyce vibrantly reveals how far we have sunk in two millennia. Leopold Bloom would have slain his wife's lover Blazes Boylan, if he were truly Ulysses. Instead, he plans a day out of the house so as not to interfere with his wife's affair.

Molly Bloom is faithless in marriage despite an ever present, doting, uxorious husband. Penelope waited for many years, rejecting the constant barrage of suitors, whom Ulysses returned to slay.

Leopold Bloom is to the hero Ulysses what Supreme Court Justice Clarence Thomas and his arch conservative ilk are to the ennobling 1971 Griggs Supreme Court decision. We have sunk from a nation of ideals to a nation in denial. We lie to ourselves if we deny that our current credentials driven society is fair. Ana Chireno sees "systemic inequality and the possibility of change." Do you? Ana's degree in philosophy has served her well. The Sigfluence Generation has to transform our credentials driven economy. The Griggs Decision threatened a great many people who benefited from unexamined credentialing – notably colleges and professional societies. We cannot expect the present arch conservative Supreme Court to insist upon heightened fairness and validity in job credentialing. However, the time will come when the Sigfluence Generation will eventually take leadership positions in education, law, the professions and the Supreme Court.

The first step in remedying our systemic American inequality is to stop lying. The opportunity to land good jobs must be made available to the economically disadvantaged. Professional societies have to admit that their role has been largely one of credentialing, and colleges have to better serve all their students - not just the academically and financially elite.

Tier 3 – The Lucky Few College Graduates Who Obtain College Related Jobs

A fortunate few are finding high paying college related jobs upon graduation. Their success belies the lie – get a good education, then you get a good job. They got a good education; they secured good jobs.

In Southeast Michigan, near Detroit with its 13.3 unemployment rate, Kent Niederhofer cannot find enough mechanical engineers to work for him. Mr. Niederhofer is the President of an engineering consultancy that designs sports' cars, huge wind turbines, and unmanned aerial vehicles.

General Electric is looking to expand its Appliance Park along with three other "centers of excellence" in refrigeration technologies, and plans to invest $1 billion that will create 1300 jobs over the next four years.

Deloitte, the world's largest professional services firm, is scouring college campuses for tax specialists, lawyers, auditors, and Millennials, who can be taught to solve emerging business problems.

Our great recession created a deep hole that may take years to climb out of. Nariman Behravesh, a chief economist for Global Insight, believes it may take until 2015 for America to return to a 6% unemployment rate – the rate economists call full employment. Technology is expected to lead our recovery. Mathematicians, biomedical engineers, network systems, and data analysts will be the vanguard of our recovery and future.

GE is focused on American jobs based on a conversion to lean manufacturing. At future GE plants, engineers, suppliers, labor, marketing, and salespeople will work on new products from concept through production. Across the United States unit labor costs have fallen; America is getting more competitive in high-end manufacturing.[25]

Credentials

The fortunate few, who excel in mechanical engineering, accounting, tax specialization, and Actuarial Science, are finding employment. They fulfill their college requirements (or pass the Actuarial tests), obtain a coveted credential, and thrive. Sadly, this is the extreme minority of college graduates. Ana, with her Stony Brook philosophy degree, will likely have to return to graduate school to earn marketable job skills. In a century or two, professional societies may be forced by an enlightened Supreme Court, to develop credentials that are valid for satisfactory job functioning. According to Carl Bankston III, the past 50 years of American education has held the view that the U.S. needs more college graduates and we need to increase college graduation rates. He argues that veterans' educational benefits coupled with Baby Boomers flocking to college in record numbers reinforced the assumption that everyone should have post secondary schooling.

For over 50 years, American colleges have steadily produced an increasing number of degrees. However, the demand for these degrees has not kept pace with the increased credentialing of America. We have created a credentials dominated society.

Degrees and credentials, according to Bankston, have become so common that students may need to attend elite private colleges in order to obtain highly sought after jobs. Of course, we are now talking about elite college graduates who have earned an elite degree from an elite college – a very small minority.

Charles Murray argues that our push toward universal college degrees ignores variations in aptitude. Everyone should not attend college.[26] My plumber makes a great deal more than I do. Again, 18 year olds need a Strong Interest Test and an hour of career counseling. A modest investment of $150 in career guidance could help to transform employment in America.

Presently, college institutionalizes disadvantage by the bankruptcy of remedial education, curriculum that has no relation to the students' future personal or professional life, and subservience to the interests of professional societies.

I did not start my career with a political bias. I was interested in sports, math, and girls. It was only after years of teaching at a Savage Inequality junior high school coupled with earning a doctorate from Columbia (emphasis Statistics and Educational/Psychological Measurement) that I recognized the abuse of power by the professional societies. These fraternities create covertly biased professional requirements that exclude the poor.

College is essential for most Americans to take part in the American dream. However, there is no guarantee that college graduates will move into better jobs as our economy improves. Our income inequality is a reflection of our lack of concern for the poor. Economists Thomas P. Pieketty and Emmanuel Suez showed that the richest 1% of American households (over $370,000 per year) received 21% of income in 2008.[27] This coincides with Dr. Reich's findings, reported in his book, *Aftershock.*

A fortunate few graduate college with a degree that is in demand. Their future is set. However, if you are not an engineer, a lawyer with an Ivy League degree, or a similarly credentialed professional, your economic future is precarious. Executives, bankers, traders, and other exemplars of greed are either unwilling or incapable of sharing. But the Sigfluence Generation will be occupying seats of power and privilege in the 21st century. They could transform the workplace with a focus on fairness and sigfluence.

A Good Job

Note that we have not yet defined a "good job." This was deliberate. A "good job" is a job that fulfills your Need and Potential for Sigfluence. You certainly need enough money for food and shelter, but you do not need that Mc Mansion. A small house may fit your needs just fine. The more money you make, the more money you believe you need. Viktor Frankl (in the *Unheard Cry for Meaning*) wrote that materialistic obsessions are often times diversions from living a meaningful life. I agree with Dr. Frankl, but we also have to define meaning in terms of the sigfluence we affect toward others. Visit my website sigfluence.com. Download my 8th book, *The Sigfluence Generation,* for free. I am counting on our Millennials to redefine status. America needs a sigfluence makeover. Job esteem and money have little connection with leading a satisfying life. On our death beds, it is unlikely that we will lament the extra $200,000 we might have earned working weekends and completely neglecting family. Rather, we will reflect on whether we have lived up to our Potential for Sigfluence.

Summary For You To Get a Good Job

1) Take a Strong Interest Test and have it interpreted by a certified counselor.

2) Pursue post-secondary education continuously whether you are training to become a nurse, plumber, or engineer. A bachelor's degree takes a lot of energy – 120 credits. Typically, a master's degree only requires 30-36 credits. Stay in college or technical training continuously. You will live longer and better.

3) Define "a good job" as a job where you make enough money to provide for your family and, most importantly, you fulfill an innate Need and Potential to Affect Sigfluence.

Advice for Colleges and Professional Societies

How one treats the weak and disenfranchised is a reflection of one's character, so honor the economically disadvantaged. Examine your requirements. Scrutinize your credentialing. Tear down the artificial and invalid obstacles that unfairly exclude otherwise qualified individuals from your college degree or your professional job. We may have to wait 100 years for the Supreme Court to promote equity in America and attack systemic inequality.

Carl Jung counseled individuals to develop themselves, believing that this would improve the world one individual at a time. It is imperative for us to explore how our unique set of gifts can translate into service of others.

The Sigfluence Generation can positively transform America into a more connected nation. Colleges, universities, and professional societies have to face the role they have played in perpetuating poverty. The Carnegie Foundation, with stars like Uri Treisman, should provide a new and enlightened direction to dramatically increase the college graduation rate of the economically disadvantaged. This is a major first step. Let the 21st century be one of connection, caring, and sharing. I may not live to see it, but we are going to be a more caring and sharing nation.

LIE 7 – Education and Values and Religion Do Not Mix

Values

You want to raise your child with the proper values. Religion teaches values. You want teachers who embrace proper values.

But, what exactly are values? Is there a difference between Conservative and Liberal values? Does Secretary of State Hillary Clinton share the same values as Rush Limbaugh? Do pro-choice and pro-life represent the same values? We use the term values to promote our value system, unconsciously assuming our values are a priori correct, others a priori wrong.

Colleges advertise their education as value oriented. We project our values onto the college mission and assume that our values are being embraced by the college.

Abraham Maslow, a pioneer in humanistic psychology, considers the ultimate disease of our time to be "valuelessness." However, he neglects to clarify what universal values we should embrace.

In educational psychology, the muddle over values continues. We learn that values are more fundamental than interests. The *Super Work Values Inventory* measures sixteen distinct personal values. For example, you may score high on creativity and be encouraged to take a job where you invent new things.

The closest value to sigfluence in Dr. Super's test (he is the world leader in researching values) is altruism. Altruism would be part of work where you are helping others.[28]

Years ago I attended a seminar on values led by Dr. Super. He told us that interests and values had such high correlations that from a research perspective they were virtually the same. So follow this muddle. You want to instill the right values in your children. You want to teach them universal values. So you can simply teach your children baseball or fly fishing to promote values.

According to the research of Dr. Super interests and values are interchangeable. Altruism values, or interest in helping others, is one of 16 values. No value is considered superior to another. No wonder Dr. Maslow considers "valuelessness" to be the ultimate disease of our time. According to academic psychology, stamp collecting and helping others are simply reflections of different and equal value systems. The winner of the muddle sweepstakes is "values."

The academic world is partially to blame for this mess. Sigfluence is a universal value that is a neglected need for humans. Sigfluence should be highlighted by college and K-12 education as a universal value and a fundamental human need. The term value should be outlawed by the academic world and replaced by the unambiguous word – interest. Altruism is not a value. Helping others is not an interest. Altruism and helping others are fundamental human needs.

Religion

Our founding fathers showed great wisdom in the separation of church and state. They foresaw the danger in instituting a state religion and for centuries we have operated with a strict demarcation between public funding of religious schools. With the religious diversity that America honors and embraces, there is little chance that the United States will ever become a theocracy. The time is right for the Sigfluence Generation to seize the potential of religion to unite, not divide. Recently, the New York Times devoted an entire page to the esteemed leaders in Christianity, Judaism, Islam, and Buddhism signing of a document that formally united the world's great religions through their common love of neighbor and God.

Love of Neighbor

When the New York Times advertisement of religious unity was published, I was struck that the love of God and love of neighbor were the only bridges between the different faiths. My minister, Rev. DeHoff, enlightened me that love of neighbor was not a small thing. Let us explore active religious love of neighbor.

Christianity

I often feel that my early immersion in Christianity and the excellence of my elementary school Catholic education inspired me toward a career in teaching – serving others. Teaching is all about service and the great world religions are united by service - love of neighbor. During the 21st century, we need more explicit demonstrations of love of neighbor between different religions. We must move from promoting religious tolerance to inspiring religious altruism toward people of different faiths.

Mother Teresa is an exemplar of active love of neighbor. She described her calling:

> "...at the feet of our Lady of Letnice where I first heard the divine call, convincing me to serve God and to devote myself to His service."

Mother Teresa recalled her "call within a call" to renounce teaching as a Loreto Sister and serve the poorest of the poor. Her words:

> "I felt that Jesus wanted me to serve Him among the poorest of the poor, the uncared for, the slum dwellers, the abandoned, the homeless. Jesus invited me to serve Him and follow Him in actual poverty, to practice a kind of life that would make me similar to the needy in whom He was present, suffered and loved."[29]

Mother Teresa is one of the most beloved people of our time. Her establishment of worldwide ministries to the poor is the epitome of an active love of neighbor. Psychology might say that Mother Teresa satisfied a "helping interest" or "altruist value." They might say that Mother Teresa is simply a person endowed with an extraordinarily high interest in making a positive difference. Psychology has to rewrite all its textbooks.

Sigfluence is a fundamental need of all humans. Mother Teresa serves as an example for us to follow.

It took Bill Gates and Warren Buffett a long time to become leaders in philanthropy. It would be advantageous for the Sigfluence Generation to turn to Mother Teresa as a model for spiritual fulfillment. Millennials could be encouraged to make lots of money. Then they will have the resources to help the less fortunate. We can follow the philanthropic leadership of Bill Gates and Warren Buffett, who have now found great Potential to affect sigfluence.

Accedie

In one of his many brilliant sermons, Rev. DeHoff edified us as to one of the deadliest sins – accedie. Accedie is not living up to the law of God and could be termed spiritual sloth. Our denial of the educational lies that pervade America is accedie. Our not caring about the less fortunate is accedie. In Ephesians: 5:6-14:

> "Live as children of light - ...try to find out what is pleasing to the Lord. Take no part in the unfruitful works of darkness, but instead expose them."

Our lack of caring for others is accedie. Our willingness to live in gated communities or Manhattan opulence, while accepting the embarrassingly high levels of incarceration of minorities, is accedie.

Helping others is hard work. Do not assume that an active spiritual love is without problems. In Luis Bunuel's classic film Viridiana, the naïve ex-novitiate Viridiana invited the poor and crippled to a banquet. She acted with little insight or caution and suffered grave consequences because of unreflective helping. Active love of neighbor will have its pitfalls, but the status quo of denial, accedie, and greed is unsustainable.

Reverend DeHoff believes that the educational problems of the poor are "a religious issue." It should be a major concern of Christians, one which cannot be solved by the Bible or prayer. Dr. DeHoff believes that the church should play a critical role in attacking the cause of

America's societal problems. Sadly, we have not yet started a comprehensive delivery of excellent K-16 education for the economically disadvantaged. Affluent communities are able to hire highly qualified teachers, develop model curriculum, and ensure that their parental privilege is passed on to their children through quality education. America has to start providing an equal education to those who are presently underserved.

Pastor DeHoff sagely advises us that American education is a reflection of our society and what we value. According to DeHoff the cutbacks in education, exemplified by Superintendent Pierorazio's tragic budget shortfall in Yonkers, NY, are

> "wrong headed... we spend millions (billions) on new stadia while Yonkers lays off hundreds of vital new teachers."

Pastor DeHoff went on to criticize the industrial-prison complex:

> "We build more prisons to feed (the prison) industry."

Pastor DeHoff also believes that national career testing at age 18 could help people find more meaningful careers. He notes that little is done in America to open the eyes of young people to the myriad of career directions. Dr. DeHoff's son rejected the engineering direction that his early career tests showed. However, after earning degrees in music and business, he became an expert in injection molding - an esoteric specialty that suited his engineering aptitude. Too many people who go to college and fail would have thrived in a trade. It is a wonder that anyone achieves a meaningful career given the dearth of career guidance in American education.

Pastor DeHoff closes with advice similar to the counsel of Carl Jung: "Take care of yourself. Then you can love your neighbor." However, he cautions us to avoid becoming enablers. At Alcoholics Anonymous each person is responsible for his/her cure. We have to walk a tightrope between neglect and enabling.

Judaism

Rabbi Mark Sameth generously granted me an interview in June of 2011. Rabbi Sameth, who has served as Rabbi for Pleasantville since 1998, leads a meditation session every week. Meditation is a great source of spiritual renewal in our distracted world. According to Rabbi Sameth, the poor economy along with the hyped up speed of daily life, are two of the tough challenges facing people today.

Maggie Jackson has written a provocative book, *Distracted*, which explores our eroding capacity for intimacy, wisdom, and cultural progress. Our young people are adrift in 50 million websites, 75 million blogs, and superficial Google searches, and they desperately need focus and connection. Meditation can enhance focus, but Sigfluence is the key to connection.

Rabbi Sameth described a very active program of social outreach at his synagogue, which includes delivering food to the Pleasantville food pantry, driving to New York City to feed frail Jews on Jewish holidays, as well as participating in international food relief.

Rabbi Sameth continued:

"Yesterday the back of the sanctuary was filled with food in partnership with (the local) mosque. Jews and Muslims are working together. We are all one family. Caring for our fellow human beings is a concern that unites us."

He is describing the type of active, joint, highly visible partnership between Jews and Muslims that is essential to a peaceful 21st century.

Rabbi Sameth described Judaism as having a commitment to being in the world. Judaism is focused on TIKKUN ALAM – "Repair of the World." This key concept in Judaism is fundamental to social action and charity. He also cited a deep Jewish commitment to teaching.

Judaism hopes to cultivate caring, responsible citizens who will "repair the world."

The world needs a lot of repair and education is arguably the best long-term solution to "repair of the world," but we have to face the lies that pervade American education.

Rabbi Sameth loved the coinage of my new word – sigfluence. He cited the Rabbis of the Talmud:

"If you teach someone, it is as if you have sired them."

This is reverence for teaching, a reverence America deeply needs. New York State Teacher of the Year (2008) Richard Ognibene decried New York State's heightened emphasis on standardized tests to evaluate teachers in the following:

"Using standardized tests as 40% of a teacher's evaluation will be bad for students and teachers alike....what we do in school is incredibly complex and much of it cannot be measured with a #2 pencil."

America needs reverence for teaching (Rabbi Sameth) and greater reliance and faith in the world's leading expert on your child's educational growth – the teacher (Richard Ognibene). The sigfluence of a teacher may take years to be appreciated because the most important dimensions of teaching are long-term and elude annual teacher evaluations.

Rabbi Sameth saw sigfluence as a meme – the cultural equivalent of a gene. When we put an idea into the world, like compassion, love of neighbor, or sigfluence, they act in the meme pool like genes in the gene pool. Sometimes they become very powerful.

The meme that focuses on our remedy of Lie 7 is that religions have to work together in active and highly visible partnership in order to share a more peaceful and harmonious 21st century. Love of neighbor has to go from mere tolerance to active sharing and caring. Rabbi Sameth instructed us that:

> "Faith leads to active involvement....During the Civil Rights era, (Judaism) opposed separate but equal and encouraged getting involved with social causes."

Dr. DeHoff's sermon on accedie synergizes neatly with Rabbi Sameth's recognition that faith leads to active involvement. The Gospel of James instructs us that deeds are a natural consequence of faith. If you have faith, then you will have deeds. If you lack deeds, then you lack faith. Deeds and active involvement in the "repair of the world" are foundational to Christianity and Judaism. Spiritual foundation, common to all religions, must infuse education and transform education from its credentialing role to one of nurturing and caring.

Islam

9-11, the great American tragedy of the 21st century, affected every aspect of American life. On that day we learned that evil knows no limit. Osama Bin Laden convinced a great many impressionable Muslims that Christians were dedicated to wiping out Muslims. Eboo Patel, one of the world's visionary young leaders dedicated to promoting religious unity, compared Bin Laden with Evangelist Pat Robertson. Dr. Patel believes that Pat Robertson promotes the same concept in reverse, which is the idea that Muslims want to destroy Christians.

Dr. Patel believes that the 21st century will be shaped by the question of the faith line, just as African American scholar W.F. DuBois believes the 20th century was shaped by the color line.[30]

Eboo Patel fiercely advocates a proactive cooperation between the different faiths. He observes that Bin Laden was an effective youth organizer to preach hatred and terror. Dr. Patel has proven to be an extraordinarily gifted youth organizer to preach religious unity. In his words:

"To see the other side, to defend another people, not despite your tradition, but because of it, is the heart of pluralism...We have to save each other. It's the only way to save ourselves."[31]

Norwegian madman Anders Breivik, obsessed by what he saw as the threat of multiculturalism to the "culture and patriotic values of his country," recently assassinated at least 92 innocents.[32] Like Hitler, he perverted the Christian message of love of neighbor. Lunatics like Bin Laden and Breivik, get headlines, but good will ultimately prevail. Muslims and Christians gathered together on March 26, 2011 to celebrate the 4th annual Interfaith Program celebrating religious unity and a universal code of morality, good conduct, and love of neighbor.[33] For every Breivik, the world has millions of normal, decent citizens, committed to living purposeful lives.

A top Vatican official said that a letter from 138 Muslim clerics, scholars, and intellectuals from all branches of Islam "represents a very encouraging sign because it shows that goodwill and dialogue are capable of overcoming prejudices."

Anglican Archbishop Rowan Williams commented on the letter:

"(the) theological basis of the letter....to vie with each other only in righteousness and good works; to respect each other, be fair, just and kind to each other and live in sincere peace, harmony, and mutual good will, are indicative of the kind of relationship for which we yearn in all parts of the world, and especially where Christians and Muslims live together."[34]

Archbishop Williams leads the 77 million members of the Anglican Community. The Vatican represents several hundred million Roman Catholics. The great religions preach love. Fanatics like Bin Laden and Breivik make splashy and trashy headlines. But the Sigfluence Generation is poised to foster religious unity and connection – not terrorism and division.

Buddhism

Although Buddhism does not embrace a higher power (God), it regards the individual as the pivotal force of change within the interdependent network of life. The individual becomes the source of ultimate wisdom of the human condition.[35]

Buddhism has millions of followers and has a spiritual focus. An exemplar of Buddhism and spiritual mentor for us all is the Dalai Lama. The Dalai Lama's words are in harmony with the world's great religions. He advises us:

> "the most important thing is another level of spirituality without religious faith, which is simply to be a good human being – thoughtful, honest, warm-hearted...humanity cannot survive without that."[36]

The Dalai Lama described himself as a "humble Buddhist monk." He travels the world as an ambassador of peace and harmony. He has received the Nobel Peace Prize and has been recognized as one of the world's most influential people.

Schools must reveal the commonality among the world's religions. After the family, schools are the world's most influential institutions. If Andres Breivik had been educated as to the love of neighbor inherent in all religions and the need for tolerance and religious unity, the Norway tragedy could have been averted. Fifty years ago the election of a Black American President was unthinkable. In a very haphazard, desultory fashion we are moving towards an evolved and enlightened nation. Schools and religious harmony mix, and mix well. In time America will honor the connection and love of neighbor intrinsic to the great religions of the world.

LIE 8 – Poor Parents Do Not Care About Their Children's Education

This is a 100% unadulterated, unequivocal lie. For 13 ½ years of my first 15 years in teaching, I taught in Savage Inequality schools. Well over 90% of the students had cards for free lunch. Lunch and breakfast might have been the only nutritious meals that those students received.

When I worked as a math teacher, and later as a guidance counselor, I visited countless homes and met with hundreds of parents. Not one single parent was unconcerned about his/her child's progress. Often times the parents (or single parent) worked two low wage jobs and had little emotional resources left for active engagement with the school, but they all still cared about their children's education. They wanted a better life for their children - 100% of them.

Frequently, the parents were unaware of the credit requirements for high school graduation or courses that were beneficial for college preparation. Even highly educated parents had to be informed of educational requirements for college or high school graduation. Trivial information, from a guidance perspective, was revelatory to both parents of privilege and parents from economically disadvantaged environments. But both sets of parents cared equally about the education of their children.

Dr. Joseph Hankin, who recently celebrated his fortieth year as President of Westchester Community College, also believes that it is a lie that parents from lower socioeconomic backgrounds do not care. He states that:

"If (poor) parents had optimal resources, life would be different... (they often have) two jobs and are tired parents."

Dr. Hankin believes (as I do) that Americans have lost their way. But we must rid education of insidious lies. Poor parents care deeply.

71

Gretchen Loase also believes that poor parents care deeply about education and that America needs to improve the quality of education at the elementary and junior high school level. College is too late to catch up.

Ms. Loase states that child care should be readily available for economically disadvantaged mothers so that (with fair wages) they can afford higher education, work reasonable hours, and provide a model for their economically disadvantaged children.

Professor Melvin Butts echoes these sentiments. He observes that raising a family is a challenge for two parents, let alone a single parent. The single parent has virtually no time to help their children with homework or extracurricular activities. Professor Butts assumes loco parentis responsibilities as part of the after school tutorial program he innovated at Redeemer Church in the Bronx. Professor Butts reflects on faith and helping:

"I have been privileged by our Lord and Savior to achieve things that I could not have achieved alone. I feel an obligation to do what I can to help others."

Through his work at Redeemer Church, Professor Butts receives the same joy that I received from innovating the Responsibility Training program for students who were left back. Poor parents care, but they need help from us to empower their children with the post-secondary degree that will lead to a fruitful career. America has to replicate Professor Butts' tutorial in other communities, all across the nation. It is not parental concern that is lacking, but rather a lack of national will to transform education and opportunity.

Superintendent Bernard Pierorazio also knows that poor parents uniformly care. He cited forty parents who recently marched on Yonkers City Hall, protesting the catastrophic cuts in his education budget. One parent movingly appealed:

"I don't have real estate or money. The only thing I can provide is education, and you can't take it away."

72

This exemplary poor parent expressed touching concern for his children's education. The idea that poor parents care deeply about their child's education received unanimous support from everyone I interviewed for this book – way over 100 years of pooled experience. If you are still not convinced, watch *Waiting for Superman*, an award winning documentary about Geoffrey Canada's revolutionary charter school in Harlem, where I delivered a College Success Seminar to the entire 9th grade last year. The dedication of the faculty, the wonderful relation between teachers and students, and our enthusiastic reception was one of my career highlights. But half of the parents who apply for the Harlem Promise Academy are turned down. While you view *Waiting for Superman* scrutinize the tears streaming down the faces of the parents whose children lost the lottery to enter Promise Academy.

Poor parents care deeply. It is time to transform America through education.

Parent Involvement

Our guides unanimously support the thesis that poor parents care deeply about the education of their children. Research also consistently demonstrates the powerful positive relationship between family involvement and student success. Unfortunately, researchers consider current education policies as "creating random acts of family involvement."[37] American education has to innovate continuous strategies to foster family involvement. Success in fostering family involvement, especially for low income families, may prove sigfluential in enhancing both the high school and post-secondary graduation rates of economically disadvantaged children.

The United States Department of Education also cites overwhelming evidence correlating family involvement and student success.[38]Family involvement is fundamental to school success, especially for low income children. It is a no brainer. Get poor parents actively involved.

However, it is not as easy as it sounds. As a young, naïve, idealistic guidance counselor at Yonkers High

73

School, I singlehandedly moved the PTA, administration, and guidance faculty to plan a parents' night to answer questions, present an overview of college planning, and to initiate school-family connections for several thousand poor families. The PTA sent out 2500 letters inviting families to our evening session. I was chided by some experienced colleagues who felt that I was wasting their time and mine. Unfortunately, they were right. Our fifteen counselors dramatically outnumbered the parents who attended. I am not an expert on the literature on family involvement, but it takes significant educational resources to create family connections with school. However, we can share best practices and try to improve from our current "random acts of family involvement."

LIE 9 – We Can Do Nothing To Transform Education

We can transform American education. Here are nine ideas for starters:

1) Fund Exemplary Programs like Head Start

Superintendent Pierorazio found that his pre-kindergarten innovation provided a huge boost to long-term school achievement. The majority of his four year old students were reading by January in pre-K. Bernard believes that this translated into a 90% high school graduation rate. He lamented that things may lapse to a 40-50% high school graduation rate with no pre-K. A modest initial investment in early education pays huge dividends long-term. More people will graduate high school, earn post-secondary degrees, and contribute to jobs and to the economy if funding is increased for early education programs.

2) Give Teachers Esteem

It is time to honor teachers with the high esteem they deserve. My life has been sigfluenced by my two wonderful 9th grade Algebra teachers, Mary O'Connor Reynolds and Louis Rotando. It took many years for me to recognize the sigfluence Mary and Lou imparted to me.

Again, New York State Teacher of the Year (2008) Richard Ognibene said it perfectly:

"What we (teachers) do in schools is incredibly complex and much of it cannot be measured with a #2 pencil."

Supervisors and principals should adopt the servant-leader model of President Joseph Hankin. Dr. Hankin devotes his professional life to the development of staff and faculty, so that we can better serve the students. Spend less money on statistical tests and more money where teachers believe the students will benefit. I am an expert in Statistics and Educational Measurement. Check out my website sigfluence.com. Scrutinize my credentials. Educational testing is beset with invalid tests, unreliable measurement, and obfuscation intended to deceive the public. We need tests to identify big problems, but we need to rely upon teachers to provide solutions.

3) Explore Curriculum

How did you do on the Simplex Method? Imagine if your job were on the line based on mastery of this algorithm. For the 52% of chronic failures in College Algebra at State University Y, they never got their bachelor's degree or a professional job, due to College Algebra and the dreaded Simplex Method.

Power corrupts, and absolute power corrupts absolutely. Colleges have absolute power. Professors and departments define required curriculum and it is hopeless to expect them to change. Or is it?

My article in the 2007 Mathematical Association of America's publication, Focus, called for Statistics to be the new math. Statistics is practical, not highly dependent upon a facility in arithmetic and algebra, and is invaluable in one's personal and professional life. Dozens of professors and teachers across the United States and Canada requested my 90 page book -*Essential Statistics with the* TI83 *Calculator.* Perhaps 10 colleges and high schools have adopted my student-centered approach to college mathematics. 10 down, thousands to go.

On a positive note, the Carnegie Foundation with the leadership of superstar Professor Uri Treisman appears to be following or converging on my recommended curriculum transformation to Statistics. In "Make Math a Gateway, not a Gatekeeper," Carnegie President Anthony Bryk and Professor Treisman implored community colleges (and all concerned educators) "to build new pathways worthy of mathematics, worthy of their students, and worthy of their institutional missions."[39] They support my 2007 direction published in Focus and recommend Statistics to become the pathway to college and professional success for our students.

Statistics is the minimum mathematics that colleges should require for all students. Colleges should become talent hunters for students with mathematics aptitude. Any student from a normal high school environment, who scores 600 or better on the Mathematics SAT Test, should be encouraged to take the college mathematics sequence of: College Algebra - Trigonometry, Calculus 1, Calculus 2, Calculus 3, and beyond. For students from economically disadvantaged systems, a mathematics SAT score of 500 indicates math talent that should be encouraged and nurtured.

In former Reserve Chairman Dr. Alan Greenspan's autobiography, he identifies our nation's weakness in mathematics and science as a more serious, long-term threat to America than terrorism. Our race to the bottom in education, evidenced by recent Congressional budget cuts, suggests that we are mired in short-term thinking. Education is the intellectual infrastructure upon which our future economy builds, and it is crumbling.

4) Support Education Budgets

If we eviscerate the education of the poor, we dramatically lower the high school and post-secondary graduation prospects for poor children. Our national incarceration rate makes other nations look good. We can transform systemic inequality one school budget at a time. A mind is a terrible thing to waste. Imagine the lost human potential in Yonkers, if the school budget is not restored and graduation rates are cut in half.

Americans have a short-term mentality. We elect presidents for four year terms. Earnings from companies, whose stocks we own, are reported every three months. America needs a long-term focus.

The citizens, who vote for school budgets, are cut off from the effects of their vote. We need to highlight the connection between school budgets and sigfluence. Superintendent Pierorazio is wounded by the dire long-term consequences of losing exemplary programs like Pre-

K. Skilled politicians feed our denial and skillfully absolve
us from any responsibility for human suffering. America
has a huge job ahead of it if we are going to transform
education in the 21st century. The Sigfluence Generation
is up to the job, but our Millennials need mentorship from
the Baby Boomers so as not to repeat their mistakes.

5) Slowly Extricate Yourself from Denial

President Obama's lie about becoming #1 in the world
in college graduation rates by 2020 feeds our denial. We
do not want to know that we play a significant role in
perpetuating poverty and privilege in America.

All children should have access to a quality education,
but they don't. I am still waiting to be reimbursed for our
family money that went to pay for books that the New York
public schools never provided.

America has been like an ostrich with its head in the
sand in terms of addressing how poor children may not
even get proper textbooks, while privileged children get the
latest and best learning materials. We perpetuate systemic
inequality. Education is a reflection of our neglect.

6) Get Involved

Professor Melvin Butts innovated an exemplary tutorial
program at Redeemer Church in the Bronx. It is a model
for family involvement. If you commit to making a
difference, the rewards are great. In the words of Professor
Butts:

> "I receive a constant joy from helping. It is not the
> purpose but it is a reward. Society benefits from
> this service."

I derived the same constant joy from delivering five
College Success Seminars to over 1000 economically
disadvantaged students from Yonkers, Mount Vernon and
Harlem. Given the number of phone calls and emails that
Professor Butts and I have made, we should have reached
10,000 students by now. But, the real world presents

constant roadblocks to sigfluence. Be persistent. It is worth it.

As a math professor, I channeled math and my counseling background into a College Success Seminar. I was then able to innovate College Statistics to an appreciative and marvelous group of students at Riverside High School last year. We all have talents that should be shared. Reflect on how to share your talents. Poverty in America can be ameliorated. Post-secondary graduation rates in America can be improved, one student at a time.

Our current educational system has a lot in common with cancer treatment. Some students need modest educational modifications, while others require continuous and creative strategies. America has a dark side and a bright side. It is the land of opportunity for poor kids like me, who were able to overcome economic disadvantage. But I was lucky to have a high math aptitude. Somehow, we have to provide education to poor children and ensure that they do not give up, abandon hope, and drain society. One of our greatest losses is the loss of Potential for Sigfluence for students who fall out of our educational system. America will save a lot of money in the long run just by funding exemplary programs like pre-K. It is much harder to combat hopelessness and failure later on. Catch up rarely works. We have to show continuous caring - Pre-K through post secondary. Otherwise we lose vast human potential.

7) Foster Connections

Gretchen Loase and Dr. Hankin applaud the wonderful achievement of TRIO students at Westchester Community College. TRIO's retention rate appears to double the historical rate by extensive caring, tutoring, and a family atmosphere.

Dr. Hankin believes that connections lead to student success, and Gretchen completely agrees. She builds these connections. TRIO students become an extended family. The students care and nurture one another. They are counseled to overcome financial, scheduling, and academic problems. They are inspired by caring professionals who create and nurture positive relationships.

Low income students frequently come from single parent homes, where the parent may require two low wage jobs to survive. The parent often lacks post-secondary education. Consequently, exemplary programs, such as TRIO, provide the support that is common in middle class and affluent families. If we withdraw this support, the student fails and loses hope. Again, Ana is right. America's dark side is systemic inequality. TRIO, pre-K programs and strategies that foster parental involvement share one characteristic – INVOLVEMENT and CONNECTIONS.

When I innovated Responsibility Training three decades ago at a Savage Inequality junior high school, I recruited dozens of college students from Manhattan College and Mt. St. Vincent as tutors. Each tutor had a group of 3 or 4 students to tutor and counsel. I believed then, as I believe now, that the college students were primarily building CONNECTIONS. They inspired their students to work hard in class and do well. Poor students repay kindness with touching loyalty. When you establish trust, they want to do well in school to please you and to have a brighter future. Connections, connections, connections are fundamental to making inroads in overcoming the widespread failure of poor children K-16. Their failure mirrors our neglect. Our individual transformations will mirror America's educational transformation.

8) Professions Need to Create Valid Entrance Standards

It may surprise you that few, if any, professions scrutinize their requirements. Both the Association for Computer Machinery and the Society of Actuaries ignored my lecture and writings revealing that their job requirements had little to do with the job. Their professional requirements are designed to maintain an equilibrium between supply and demand. One of my friends, who trained to become an Actuary, told me that when an eighth grade math problem came into the Actuarial department (like using a calculator to compute a square root), the Actuaries staged a mock fight to determine who would gain the honor of answering the "advanced" question. After all, most of their work was fifth or sixth grade arithmetic.

I was surprised when I found that the discrepancy between college requirements and job demands appears to be universal. At Stanford Law School, a great number of the students show up unprepared for lectures. Silence pervades the lecture hall. One third year student commented:

> "They don't teach you to be a lawyer very well, and the theory is just incredibly shallow."[40]

Perhaps this is why they use the term "practicing lawyer." They are practicing law, learning law on the job, and we pay hundreds of dollars an hour for their practice.

What about doctors? At a Mensa (high IQ society) convention, Dr. Karl Humiston accused doctors of staying away from a health oriented approach to medicine. Dr. Humiston had the impeccable credentials of a Harvard medical degree and advanced psychiatric training. It was only after marrying a nutritionist that he discovered nutrition as a sine qua non of health. His medical training exclusively focused on pathology – not health.[41]

Please do not consider me advocating college turning into a trade-technical institution for job training. Literature and psychology may prove as beneficial to your personal and professional life as job specific training. But there has to be some scrutiny of the validity of professional training. In time, professional societies should develop alternative paths to job certification. This would ameliorate the "covert bias" against the economically disadvantaged, who typically are unable to afford the lengthy credentialing process common to all professions.

9) Religions Should Lead the Way

The Sigfluence Generation hungers for a spiritual direction in their lives. I use the word spiritual in accord with definitions one and seven from the American Heritage Dictionary (3rd edition):

1. The animating force within human beings;

7. Vivacity, vigor, or courage

Animate comes from the Indo-European root -ane, which means to breathe.[42] Love of neighbor, when manifested in tangible connections, animates. The world's great religions are united by love. We need to see more love across religious boundaries.

Visionaries, like Eboo Patel, are leading the way. Dr. Patel reminds us that Rev. Martin Luther King partnered with Rabbi Abraham Joshua Heschel for civil rights. Dr. Patel also instruct us that Mahatma Gandhi believes that Hindu-Muslim unity was as important as a free India.[43]

Dr. Patel eloquently expresses active engagement of the great faiths in overcoming injustice:

> "Islam calls upon Muslims to be courageous and compassionate in the face of injustice....the ice of silence will kill pluralism as will the fire of a suicide bomber."[44]

To buttress the vision of Dr. Patel, the Dalai Lama counsels us to develop secular ethics and become "a good human being - thoughtful, honest, warm-hearted,"[45]

The great religions must demonstrate love. His Reverence the Dalai Lama left out a key ingredient necessary for educational transformation. It is not enough to be thoughtful, honest, and warm-hearted. We need to develop ourselves and share our talents with people from other religions and backgrounds. We need to find our zone of sigfluence, where faith and spirituality animates our outreach to others. As Professor Butts eloquently expressed:

> "I receive a constant joy from helping."

If President Obama achieved nothing else by his great lie than inspiring this book and one animated reader, his misstep was not in vain.

Appendix A.

1) President of Westchester Community College – Dr. Joseph Hankin.

President Hankin has been named one of the top 100 college presidents in America by his peers. He also holds Full Professor status at Columbia University Teachers College, arguably the leading university in America in education.

President Hankin was instrumental in my professional development. I was a poor kid from Mt. Vernon. My parents had no formal college training. I feel confident with national leadership in mathematics and education, thanks to the confidence he built in me and many others.

2) Yonkers Superintendent of Schools, Bernard P. Pierorazio.

Superintendent Pierorazio was recently named New York State School Superintendent of the Year. Bernard was one of the finest teachers I ever had the honor to teach with. Yonkers could not be better served.

3) Professor Melvin Butts.

Professor Butts has taught math with me at Concordia College for the past five years. We have been partners during the past three years in an outreach program to high schools with a high proportion of the economically disadvantaged. We have delivered 90 minute College Success Seminars to over 1,000 students from Yonkers, Mt. Vernon and Harlem. The students have given us rave evaluations, but most administrators have thwarted our efforts to expand and reach more students. One has to have a little Don Quixote of idealism to overcome the obstacles that hinder progress in education. Fortunately Melvin Butts is the man for the job. He has served as a leader in three careers. He was a battalion Commander of 1400 as Colonel of the Army Corps of Engineers. Melvin served as a Professor of Management at West Point, Dean of Business and Technology at Triton College (Chicago), and also owned a Washington, DC construction company.

Without Melvin's support and wisdom, I would not have overcome the pervasive roadblocks we encountered to finally succeed in delivering a College Success Seminar followed by the innovation of my College Statistics course at Riverside High School in Yonkers during the Spring of 2011. We had 100% success with a class of marvelous students, an exemplary master teacher Maria Rodriguez, and the complete support of Riverside High School Principal Steven Murphy and Assistant Principal Carol Baiocco

4) Principal Steven Murphy.

Principal Murphy served as principal for more than ten years at Mt. St. Michael and St. Agnes High School in New York City, Archbishop Stepinac in White Plains, and Casimir Pulaski School in Yonkers before becoming the principal of Riverside High School. He believes that an effective principal is a reflective practitioner. He also brought his experience as a guidance counselor to his perceived role as locus parentis to his students. Principal Murphy sees his students as his own children, and brings a spirit of caring and concern to each interaction with students, families, and school professionals.

5) Assistant Principal Carol Baiocco.

Melvin Butts and I would not have gotten to first base, much less hit a grand slam at Riverside High School, without the sigfluence of Carol Baiocco. I was mountain biking on the Croton Aqueduct trail near Yonkers, in despair over the dozens of ignored phone calls and e mails that Melvin and I had sent to principals in an attempt to enhance the academic performance of high school students from economic disadvantage. Despite rave reviews from students, we had not a single invitation to return and deliver our presentation to additional students.

The bike path was muddy, forcing me onto the streets of Yonkers. I soon passed Riverside High School. With bike helmet in hand, I entered Riverside High School and asked to speak with an administrator. Assistant Principal Carol Baiocco could not have been more generous and creative. She invited Melvin and me to deliver our College Success Seminar to the 11th grade. Shortly thereafter the administration of Concordia College, Dean Sherry Fraser and Dean Nakhai met with Carol and Principal Steven Murphy to innovate College Statistics at Riverside High School. We had 100% success Spring 2011 with our course. Each student earned college math credit. We want the course to go viral and reach every economically disadvantaged high school student in America.

It took me over 40 years to come up with this strategy. Over 80% of college remedial students fail to graduate within 8 years. Math is the insurmountable obstacle to college graduation, according to a 2005 report from the United States Department of Education.

President Obama, at least one college, Concordia College – NY, is on board in helping you reach the coveted #1 spot in the world in proportion of college graduates. Unfortunately, we have 3000 colleges to go.

6) Master Teacher Maria Rodriguez.

Maria Rodriguez was assigned to co-teach the Concordia College Statistics course that Melvin Butts and I planned to deliver Spring 2011. It was the first time that I had ever co-taught a class in my 42 year career. Professor Butts and I taught the class two afternoons a week. To my delight, Ms. Rodriguez followed up with three days of homework and additional exercises each week.

Principal Murphy plans to add two classes of College Statistics next year using a similar format. Maria Rodriguez predicted quite sagely that next year, we will increase the impact of our innovation, reaching 50 students, a five fold increase. Many of these students will enter college with 3 credits for College Statistics. Arguably this College Statistics credit doubles students' likelihood of college success. Ms. Rodriguez hit the nail on the head with her insight. She correctly intuits that we have to be creative and long-term in perspectives when we design strategies to sigfluence economically disadvantaged students.

7) Mrs. Gretchen Aufiero Loase.

Last, and certainly not least, I needed to interview an exemplary professional who could guide our journey from the perspective of elementary school teaching, reading, writing, and tutoring. Gretchen (my wife) started in advertising and IBM as an administrative assistant. She discovered her calling to become a teacher and earned a masters' degree in reading. Over the past two decades, Gretchen has taught elementary school in both Catholic and New York City public schools, regular grade 6 instruction in a Savage Inequality School (Read Kozol's eye opening Savage Inequality to understand why I wrote this book), a reading teacher in an affluent Westchester elementary school, and professor of Writing, Literature, Reading and English as a Second Language at Westchester Community College.

She currently loves her role as tutor of the highly successful program TRIO, which targets students with three strikes - remediation needs, first generation college student, and economic disadvantage. To our delight, TRIO saves lives and taxpayer dollars. All is not bleak on the college horizon.

ENDNOTES

1.Fyodor Dostoevsky, *Demons*, translated by Richard Pevear and Larissa Volokhonsky, (New York: Alfred Knopf, 1994), p. 652.

2.Sarah Cunnane, "Produce Eight Million Extra U.S. Graduates by 2020," *Times Higher Education*, online, August 19, 2010.

3.Scott Bland, "Obama Aims to Life College Graduation Rates, But His Tools Are Few," *Christian Science Monitor*, online, August 9, 2010.

4.Robert Reich, *Aftershock*, (New York: Alfred A. Knopf, 2010), p. 6.

5.David Brooks, "The Big Disconnect," *New York Times Week in Review*, April 26, 2011, p. A25.

6.Chris Mooney, "The Science of Why We Don't Believe Science," *Fact-Free Nation, Mother Junes Online*, June 19, 2011.

7.Jean Auel. *The Clan of the Cave Bear* (New York: Crown Publishing, 1980), pp. 92-93.

8.Christopher Jencks, et. al. *Inequality* (New York: Harper and Row, 1972), p. 193.

9.Psychological Corporation, "Memorandum to Industrial Psychologists and Executives, 1971.

10.David Leonhardt, "Top Colleges Largely For the Elite," *New York Times*, B1, May 25, 2011.

11.Richard Arum and Josipa Roksa, "Your So-Called Education," *New York Times*, May 15, 2011, Week in Review, p. 10.

12.Ulrich Trautwein and Oliver Ludtke, "Epistemological Beliefs: School Achievement and College Major," *Contemporary Educational Psychology*," July 2007, pp. 348-366.

13.Bertrand Russell, "Philosophy for Laymen," The Bertrand Russell Society, 1946.

14.Melissa Hamilton Holberg, Letter to Utne Reader, *Utne Reader*, May-June 2011, p. 6.

15.Anthony S. Bryk and Uri Treisman, "Make Math a Gateway Not a Gatekeeper," *Chronicle of Higher Education*, April 18, 2010.

16."First Year Students – Ambitious, Optimistic, and Overwhelmed," *On Campus*, May-June 2011, p. 2.

17.Ira Boudway, "More Graduates, More Job Seekers," *Bloomberg Business Week*, 6/7/10, p. 16.

18.Joseph Picard, "Is Higher Ed Too High for Americans," *IBTimes.com*, August 15, 2010.

19.Kati Haycock and Danette Gerald, "Trend: Shrinking Opportunity," *Connection*, Spring 2007, p. 15.

20.Dylan Suher, "My Tragic Starring Role," *New York Times*, Sunday Review, p. 7.

21.Ana Chirene, "Elevated by the Train," *New York Times*, Sunday Review, p. 7.

22.David Leonhardt, "Even for Cashiers, College Pays Off," *New York Times*, Sunday Review, June 26, 2011, p. 3.

23.Catherine Rampell, "Many With New College Degree Find the Job Market Humbling," *New York Times*, May 19, 2011, Front Page.

24. Psychological Corporation, "Memorandum to Industrial Psychologists and Personnel Executives," 1971.

25. Bill Saporito and Deirdre Van Dyk, "Where the Jobs Are," *Time*, Jan. 17, 2011, p. 26-35.

26. Carl Bankston III, "The Mass Production of Credentials," *Independent Review*, Winter 2011, pp. 325-249.

27. "Jobs and Inequality," *Editorial Desk*, Dec. 14, 2010, Section A.

28. Donald E. Super, *Manual for the Work Values Inventory* (Boston: Houghton Mifflin, 1970), pp. 4-10.

29. J. Gonzalez Balado and Janet Playfoot (eds.) *My Life for the Poor* (New York: Harper and Row, 1985) pp. 1-7.

30. Anthony S. Bryk and Uri Treisman, op. cit.

31. Heather B. Weiss, Suzanne M. Boufford, Beatrice L. Bridgall, and Edmund W. Gordon, "Reframing Family Involvement in Education," *Equity Matters*, Research Review No. 5, Teachers College Columbia University.

32. Eric Dearing, Holly Kreider, and Heather B, Weiss, "Increased Family Involvement in School Predicts Improved Child-Teacher Relationships and Feelings About School for Low-Income Children," *Marriage and Family Review*, Vol. 43, 2008, pp. 226-254.

33. D. Margolick, "The Trouble with America's Law Schools," *New York Times*, May 22, 1983, pp. 22-25.

34. Eboo Patel, *Acts of FaithActs of Faith* (Boston: Beacon Press, 2007), p. xv.

35. Eboo Patel, op. cit., p. 179.

36. Steven Erlanger, "Campers Tricked: Suspect Called Anti-Islam," *New York Times*, July 24, 2011.

37. "Muslims and Christians to Celebrate the 4th Annual Milad-un-Nabi Honoring the Birth of the Holy Last Messenger Muhammad," *United Muslim-Christian Forum*, March 26, 2011.

38. Eric Young, "Call for Muslim-Christian Unity 'Very Encouraging' Says Vatican Interfaith Head," *Christian Post*, Oct. 14, 2007, p. 1-2.

39. Daisaku Ikeda, "Buddhist Humanism," *Daisaku Ikeda Website*.

40. J. Wooter, "The Concilator," *New York Times Magazine*, Jan. 29, 1995, p. 28.

41. Mensa is a private society with membership based on an IQ (or equivalent measure) in the upper 2%. Dr. Humiston spoke at the New York Mensa Convention in 1984.

42. James Hollis, *The Middle Passage* (Toronto: Inner City Books, 1993), pp. 46-47.

43. Eboo Patel, op. cit., p. xvii.

44. Eboo Patel, op. cit., p. xix.

45. J. Wooter, op.cit., *New York Times Magazine*, Jan. 29, 1995, p. 28.

	DATE DUE	

15690572R00051

Made in the USA
Lexington, KY
11 June 2012